Blessings from God

Willa Wiltsie Johnson

Blessing from God
© 2011 Willa Johnson

All rights reserved. No portion of this book may be reproduced, stored in a retrieval system or transmitted in any form or by any means—electronic—mechanical—recording—photocopy—scanning, or other—without the prior written permission of the author.

Cover by Gerri Frazier

Scripture quotations used from *The Scofield Reference Bible,* King James version. Copyright renewed 1937, 1945 by Oxford University Press, New York, Inc.

Scripture quotations used from *The Holy Bible,* New International Version, Copyright © 1973, 1978, 1984 by International Bible Society, published by The Zondervan Corporation, Grand Rapids, Michigan 49506, U.S.A.

Scripture quotations used from *New American Standard Bible,* Moody Press, Chicago © The Lockman Foundation 1960, 1962, 1963, 1968, 1971, 1972, 1973, 1975

ISBN 978-1-257-12276-9

Books may be ordered through http://www.lulu.com

Printed in the United State of America

ACKNOWLEDGEMENTS

My major in college was journalism and it was useful to me during my employment years in administrative work. After retiring, I attended a writers group intending to learn how to write fiction. That wasn't my forte but I did write a story about my father's life, using notes he had written shortly before his death.

Many friends have told me how much they enjoy the essays I write for *The Christian Journal* but it was my friend, Gerri Frazier, who encouraged me to publish a book of the articles. My biggest fans now are my siblings but I am grateful to all who have encouraged me.

Willa Wiltsie Johnson

FORWARD

As a child my dream was to become a reporter. That never happened but I have managed to use my writing skills from time to time through newsletters, church bulletins and a few thousand letters to various editors.

A few years ago Chad McComas, a local pastor, was led to start a quarterly Christian free publication, *The Christian Journal.* Chad wanted to reach more people with the Good News that Jesus Christ can save and thus change a person's life. He asked me if I would like to write from a senior's point of view and I readily accepted. Since then the paper has evolved into a monthly publication. It can be read online at www.thechristianjournal.org.

After becoming a widow at age 61, I realized more each day how dependent upon the Lord I became. Being a natural born stubborn, willful, independent, opinionated person...rebellious at times...my writings are filled with convictions learned the hard way.

The articles were written over a period of several years, therefore some scriptures appear more than once.

Now, at age 85, I have decided that, if I want to leave any kind of a legacy to my family and friends, I better "get 'er done." It is my hope and prayer that you will find answers to your own life's experiences as I did in mine once I learned to fully trust in the Lord for everything! May God bless you as you travel down the highway of this earthly life.

~Willa Wiltsie Johnson

THIS BOOK IS DEDICATED TO

My son Steve & his family
My brother Lee & his family
My sister Corrine & her family
The memory of my husband, Dick
The memory of my parents,
Obe & Soph Wiltsie
My friends who have encouraged me

CONTENTS

Part One – *God's Promises*

A Real New Life	1
Ability to Endure	3
Abundance…If Only	6
ALL Authority Is Given	9
Being Confident	11
Change to What?	13
Commit Thy Way	16
Commitment to What	20
Counting My Blessings	23
Courage	28
Courage, Not Fear	31
Discerning God's Will	33
Existing Without Power	35
Fear of What? Whom?	39
Finding Inner Peace	43
Follow Me	46
Growing Up	48
Have and Have Not	50
He Restoreth My Soul	53
If Only	56
Importance of Resurrection	58
Non-Transferrable	60

One of Those Days 63
Praise the Lord! 67
Rebirth Gratitude 69
Reconcile to Whom or What? 71
Renewal of the Mind 75
Reward? Yes or No 77
Righteousness? Yes, but… 79
The Best Is Yet to Come 82
The Promise of Hope 85
True Love 89
When Generosity Really Counts 91
Why Not Sin? 93
Why Repent? 96

Part Two – *Our Part*

Acceptance…Just As I Am 98
Ah, Patience 100
A Purity 104
Be Ye Kind, One to Another 106
Breastplate of Righteousness 109
Contentment IS Possible 112
Do the Right Thing 116
Faith Is 119
Forgiving 122

Free to Serve 125

Giving Up 129

Growing in Grace 131

Growing Up, Not Out 133

Honesty IS the Best Policy 138

I Am Sorry 141

Joyful Living 145

Little Is Much 149

Looking on the Inside 153

Ministers for Christ 155

No Man Is An Island 159

No One is Pure…But 163

Obedience to God's Will 165

Peaceful Harmony 167

Reasons or Excuses 169

Reconciliation with Christ 171

Refreshing Entertainment 173

Revealed Truth 175

Setting Priorities 177

Simple Faith 179

Taking In or Giving Out? 180

The Mystery of Courage 183

The Ultimate Sacrifice 187

Thy Kingdom Come 190

To Chasten or Not 192
To Whom Honor Is Given ...….........................195
Victory Over Death 199
Victory Over Death 199
What Is Truth? ……………..............................202
What Purpose? ……………..............................205
Worship the King 209

Part One

God's Promises

A Real New Life

The smile on his face was so broad I too was smiling as I watched the drama unfold, appreciating the joy he was experiencing. You see, he had just been released from prison after serving over 10 years for murder, a charge he always refuted. He grabbed his son and as they embraced and cried, I shed tears too. He had been rescued, released, liberated and was now free to begin a fresh new life. The bad choices he made years ago were behind him.

Then, the victim's family members were shown. They weren't smiling. They were convinced he was guilty and an injustice had been done by setting him free. I then commiserated with them, knowing how I'd feel in their shoes.

Mike Huckabee interviewed a man who had committed murder at age 18. After spending his youth rebelling against authority and landing in prison, he turned his life over to Christ. As promised in the Bible, he became a "new creation" and was given a second chance just as promised in II Corinthians 5:17. ***Therefore if any man be in Christ, he is a new creature: old thing are passed away; behold, all things are become new.*** The former murderer now pastors one of the largest churches in Tennessee.

The fact is we all make mistakes, most of them when we're young and don't consider the consequences. The problem is there are consequences. Sin is sin whether we admit it or not. Some sins are more costly than others; such as, when a life is taken. A drunk driver doesn't intend to kill someone but too often that's what happens.

The beauty of Christianity is that anyone... everyone...can receive forgiveness. Yes, even a murderer. The men mentioned above are now free to change their lives for good but that will last only in this lifetime.

In order to have eternal redemption, one must accept Christ as Savior. **Salvation is found in no one else, for there is no other name under heaven given to men by which we must be saved.** (Acts 4:12) Jesus told Martha, *I am the resurrection and the life. He who believes in me will live, even though he dies; and whoever lives and believes in me will never die.* (John 11:25) Later, he added, *I am the way and the truth and the life. No one comes to the Father except through me.* (John 14:6a)

One of the hymns Fanny Crosby, who was blind, states, "Redeemed how I love to proclaim it! Redeemed by the blood of the Lamb; Redeemed thro' His infinite mercy, His child, and forever, I am." The happiest part of any worship service happens when someone is baptized into Christ, into a "new life." It is only through Christ we have the promise of real redemption.

Ability to Endure

There were five children who were visibly "stair step" ages and obviously one yet to put in an appearance which would be soon. *How in the world does a mother manage with a brood like that?* I wondered. Whenever I've seen reports on the McCaughey family in Iowa as they've grown over the years, I marvel at how the parents learned to maintain their sanity while raising their septuplets plus one. I remember that Mrs. McCaughey finally could endure the pregnancy no longer and the babies had to be delivered a little earlier than nine months. All but two are growing normally without any handicap and the other two are progressing well.

People who suffer from debilitating illnesses or losses of limbs oftentimes rise above their infirmities to go on to greater lives than they might have had without that loss. I read a story, written by a weatherman about his family who went through "stormy weather" because of illnesses. He related their experience of coping with the physical illnesses to different types of weather. I had never thought about such things in that way before but it's true. There are some kinds of weather one can prepare for but there are other events that happen suddenly and catch us unaware. Life itself is like that.

At my age, one sees a lot of older people who live with a mate who is severely ill or handicapped. From firsthand knowledge, I know that such a life takes a lot more patience and understanding than most of us are endowed with. Nevertheless, we manage to get through those experiences and are stronger and better people because of them. The hardest part for the well person is watching while a loved one deteriorates whether it's physical or mental. Many times the one who is mentally ill is not aware of what's happening and is not suffering pain. The heartache is inside the healthy one, the caregiver.

There are support groups that are ready and able to help, consisting of people who are going through the same type of experience. For me, it was easy to turn to scripture for solace. One of my favorite passages is Psalm 121. **I will lift up mine eyes unto the hills from whence cometh my help. My help cometh from the Lord which made heaven and earth.** Perhaps I chose that verse because I drove eastward to work every morning and saw the majestic mountain range before me. The chapter ends with **The Lord shall preserve thy going out and thy coming in from this time forth, and even for evermore**. What an encouragement and promise!

A day doesn't go by without remembering our troops all over the world who endure all sorts of hardships, not to mention their families left behind. I cannot begin to fathom what they endure.

A story is told about a woman in a lady's Bible study group who was given a verse from Malachi for their lesson. Malachi 3:3 says, **He**

will sit as a refiner and purifier of silver. The women were puzzled as to what this meant so she offered to find out. She called a silversmith and made an appointment to watch him at work without mentioning anything about the reason for her interest beyond her curiosity about the process of refining silver.

As she watched the silversmith, he held a piece of silver over the fire and let it heat up. He explained that, in refining silver, one needed to hold the silver in the middle of the fire where the flames were hottest to burn away all the impurities. The woman thought about God holding us in such a hot spot and thought again about the verse that says, ***He sits as a refiner and purifier of silver.***

She asked the silversmith if it was true that he had to sit there in front of the fire the whole time the silver was being refined. He answered, "Yes," that he not only had to sit there holding the silver, but he had to keep his eyes on the silver the entire time it was in the fire. If the silver was left a moment too long in the flames, it would be destroyed.

The woman was silent for a moment. Then she asked the silversmith, "How do you know when the silver is fully refined?" He smiled at her and answered, "Oh that's easy - when I see my image in it."

So, if today you are feeling the heat of the fire, remember that God has His eye on you and will keep watching you until He sees His image in you.

Abundance...If Only

Who among us hasn't thought at some time *"if only?"* I admit to being guilty. We could start with, i*f only* the Israelites had listened to Moses. Before that, *if only* the people had not strayed from God, there might not have been a devastating flood that wiped out all but eight humans. Even before that, *if only* Eve had not listened to the serpent. Just think, God made a perfect world. **And God saw every thing that he had made, and, behold, it was very good. And the evening and the morning were the sixth day.** (Genesis 1:31) Yes, it was perfect in every way and Adam and Eve could have had an abundant life forever. But they messed up.

Down through the ages of mankind, we have continued to disobey and stray from God, whining about situations and circumstances over which we have no control. How many times has the weather been blamed for havoc? Yet, man cannot control it. He can only warn against what might happen so people can prepare. In the Midwest during the springtime, most homes are tuned into either the radio or television because warnings are given about a possible tornado or flood approaching. One becomes accustomed to the sound of the electronic unit and pays little attention until the beep of the warning is heard. Then, ears perk up and you listen intently. Your life may depend upon your response.

Many other *if only* situations have become a

daily mantra. *If only* my spouse would treat me better; *if only* I had a better job; *if only* my co-workers would cooperate; *if only* I had more money; *if only* I had a better car; *if only* the gas didn't cost so much; *if only* .... The list is endless so what's all this about God promising us an abundant life?

We do not stop to think or realize that God's promises often contained some "ifs" within them. Reading through Deuteronomy 28 we learn of many conditions God gave to the Israelites. ***If thou wilt not hearken unto the voice of the Lord thy God, to observe to do all his commandments and his statues which I command thee this day; that all these curses shall come upon thee, and overtake thee.*** (vs. 15) The following verses throughout the chapter relate the dire curses *if* the people disobey.

Just as God made promises to curse those who disobeyed, he also made a promise to bless those who obeyed as we read in II Chronicles 7:14. ***If my people, which are called by my name, shall humble themselves, and pray, and seek my face, and turn from their wicked ways; then will I hear from heaven, and will forgive their sin, and will heal their land.***

In the New Testament Jesus made promises such as in John 14:13-15. ***And whatsoever ye shall ask in my name, that will I do, that the Father may be glorified in the Son. If ye shall ask any thing in my name, I will do it.***

If ye love me, keep my commandments. Another promise Jesus gave us is found in John 10:10b when he said, ***I am come that they might have life, and that they might have it more abundantly.***

We must ask ourselves, "What am I doing that is causing me not to have the abundant life Christ promised?" And then, "What can I do to change my situation?" If we can truly say we can't change the circumstances, then the only way to enjoy the abundant life in Christ is to turn everything over to him. Let him solve the problems that hinder our joy. Two of my favorite Bibles verses are found in Philippians 4:6, 7. ***Be careful for nothing; but in every thing by prayer and supplication with thanksgiving let your requests be made known unto God. And the peace of God, which passeth all understanding, shall keep your hearts and minds through Christ Jesus.*** There's the answer!

ALL Authority Is Given

If I heard it once, I heard it a million times. "You're not my boss and I don't have to mind you!" my sister would tell me quite emphatically. Being older, and blessed with a bossy nature, I naturally took it upon myself to tell her what she could or could not do. That didn't work most of the time. Truth be known I didn't have the authority. She knew it but that didn't stop me from trying to exercise it. Of course, when our brother, who was the oldest, tried ordering me around, I balked. Big time.

However, more than once God has chosen a younger sibling over older ones. Isaac was chosen instead of Ishmael, Jacob instead of Esau, Ephraim instead Manasseh, Moses over Aaron and David over his brothers.

The story of Joseph as told in Genesis is a good example of a younger sibling being given authority over his family. After his brothers sold him into slavery and he suffered humiliation and imprisonment through no fault of his, God raised him up to a position of authority. When his brothers came asking for help, Joseph realized that God had been in control all along. What a story of love and forgiveness.

The problem today seems to be that a good many parents have forsaken their God-given authority to guide and direct their children. Because of lack of training many youngsters are not taught right from wrong and thus suffer the consequences.

In the Bible we are shown several examples of ultimate authority. When the apostles Peter and John were threatened with jail a second time if they did not stop preaching about Jesus, Peter said, **We must obey God rather than man.** (Acts 5:29)

In Romans 13 we read the instructions about government and what our attitude toward it should be. The first verse states, **...there is no authority except from God, and those which exist are established by God.** Sometimes, it's difficult to accept that because we know there have been evil people in control of governments down through the ages and still are today.

The Gospel of Matthew ends by relating what Jesus told his followers before he returned to heaven. **All authority has been given to me in heaven and on earth.** He went on to say, **I am with you always, even to the end of the age.** That's our assurance. The Trinity is in control so we need not worry as long as we surrender to God's will.

Being Confident

Some people are born performers; others aren't. I've read that there are entertainers and speakers who become so nervous they are physically sick before going on stage. Then, there are those who enjoy being up front, entertaining others with their wit and talent. Bob Hope was a shy man off stage it was reported, but many servicemen will remember him as their all-time favorite. It's reported Dolly Parton has said, "I have more confidence than I do talent, and I think confidence is the main achiever of success." Quite a confession but she's right. Some people have talent but never develop the confidence to use it.

Judith Briles wrote a book entitled, *The Confidence Factor – How Self-Esteem Can Change Your Life.* (©1990) It was mainly written for women but some points she makes could apply to anyone. For instance, two facts she reported were:

- It is a myth that confidence is always gained through a supportive family environment during childhood.
- Self confidence is acquired, not inherited.

Those two statements alone explain why some people born in the ghetto manage to find a way out. We hear a lot about "self-made" people but there are no such humans, in my opinion. For years I believed my father was such a man.

After he related his life's story, it was obvious he had people helping him to achieve his goals. Of course, he did his part by working hard and proving he was worthy of their assistance.

Not only do other people help, but with God as a partner, it's impossible to fail *if we trust Him.* The poem entitled "Footprints" is a case in point. We go our way and then connect with Jesus. Something happens and there is only one set of prints. That's when Jesus carries us through whatever storms we face. Once we accept Jesus Christ as our Savior, we are never alone! Proverbs 3:26 begins with **For the Lord shall be thy confidence**. The middle verse of the King James version of the Bible, Psalm 118:8, states, **It is better to trust in the Lord than to put confidence in man**. Another favorite scripture is found in Proverbs 3:5 & 6. **Trust in the Lord with all thine heart; and lean not unto thine own understanding. In all thy ways acknowledge him and he shall direct thy paths.**

Every man or woman is human and will at sometime fail. *God never fails. Not ever!*

Change to What?

If you ask people in their twilight years what they think about "change," you might get a "Bah humbug!" response. Humans are not readily prone to changing anything. It's so much easier to stick with an old familiar routine, especially once we're set in our ways. Is it because a change is an unknown entity?

Life today consists of many changes, however. Some couples decide to change marriage partners or, they simply don't bother to go through a ceremony at all. Consequently, more children are being raised with only one parent or with multiple parents. This practice has not been good for society and certainly not for the children.

As one who resisted the change of music for church worship, I will admit that some things are harder to get used to than others. That was one of the harder changes for me personally.

What about clothing styles? Can anyone tell me what *is* the "*in*" style any more? Seems to me this is the area where one of the greatest cultural changes has occurred. We went from floor length to ankle length to below the knee length to above the knee length. Today, any length seems to be what's "in." That is, if a dress is worn. Many styles of women's clothing cover the bare necessities and that's all. Hopefully, the pendulum will swing back to decency before long. As for men, they had double-breasted suits, then single breasted; wide ties, then narrow ties. And most times now, no tie or jacket.

Oftentimes people think that changing their job will make a difference. Or, what about changing the color of one's hair? Possibly moving to another area will make things better. Making changes *is* a part of life. Some changes are necessary, but some are not.

On the other hand, modern technology has given us a whole new way of living at ease. No more outdoor privy, no more Saturday night only baths, no more wringer washing machines, to name a few passé items. Changing from a non-electric typewriter to a computer was a real blessing to me! Yet, there are those in my age bracket who still resist computer usage. They don't know what they're missing. In the 21st century, innovative inventions are the vogue and it is difficult for us old-timers to keep up. We now begin to wonder if the telephone will become totally extinct in our lifetime what with cell phones becoming the norm.

Most people enjoy the change of seasons the Good Lord gives us. Some of us live in an area where we can appreciate the variations without too much discomfort. We have the new life and abundance of springtime blossoms, the summertime activities, the gorgeous fall colors and then the pristine beauty of winter snows.

It reminds me of one's lifetime. First, the innocence and newness of what is to come, the energy and enjoyment of youth, followed by the slowing down and gratitude of the good around us and ending with the promise of the unseen beauty of what lies ahead for those who trust in the Lord.

Christmas is the season when we focus on giving gifts. The greatest gift comes from the promise our Lord gave us when He died so we might have eternal life. To obtain that eternal life, we *have* to make a change.

For God so loved the world, he gave his only begotten Son; that whosoever believeth in him shall not perish but have everlasting life. He that believeth on him is not condemned; but he that believeth not is condemned already, because he hath not believed in the name of the only begotten Son of God. (John 3:16 & 18)

What a promise! It makes me realize there is a *necessary* change for all...a *change in one's heart.*

Commit Thy Way

Watching the Arab mother on TV tell how proud she was of her son who was leaving to go out to sacrifice himself as a suicide bomber left me feeling sick, totally unable to relate to such action. She kissed him goodbye and smiled, in her mind thinking how blessed he would be in a few short hours.

People have said they don't believe the Bible because no one in his right mind would do what Abraham did. After waiting until he was 100 years old before being given the promised son, what would make him take Isaac up on a mountain top only to sacrifice him? The rest of the story tells how God provided a ram once Abraham proved his commitment to obey Him.

How many of us who call ourselves Christians are able to do what Daniel and his friends did? Do we have the kind of faith it takes to step into a fiery furnace or a lion's den? I must confess I'm not willing to be tested in that way.

Faith such as that is beyond our comprehension for the most part. Perhaps that is why Christianity has always grown the fastest in areas where there is persecution even to this day. People have nothing to lose so why not trust in the Lord? Where affluence abounds, we don't feel the need for something better.

The ones who come closest to that kind of faith and commitment, in my opinion, are missionaries who venture forth into the unknown with the sole desire to serve the Lord and bring others to the saving knowledge of Christ, come what may. They have such a burning desire to share the love of Christ with people who might not otherwise ever know, they forsake comforts we take for granted.

For one week a few years ago I had the opportunity, and privilege, to host a missionary couple from Haiti. Although Haiti means "pearl of the sea" it has become a hellhole on earth due to corruption. Voodooism is the accepted religion. There people still practice that heinous crime of burning babies to appease their gods. When I saw photos of charred babies, it was impossible for me to understand how any human could believe in such worship.

We now have missionaries here in America because there is such a vast need within our borders. Every day there is news about the various degrees of evil taking place. Random shootings, vandalism, child abuse, murder...you name it. We have become a nation in dire need of a turnaround. It's true there is always good to come out of every tragedy. Since 9/11/2001, there have been many converts to Christianity. People have been able to find comfort, love and peace by embracing Christ. What a pity it takes such evil acts to bring us to our senses.

Think of the dedication and commitment of people who do not accept Christianity. They give their all, every effort of their being, to further the cause in which they believe. If Christians were as dedicated, we would be making much more progress than we are.

Much of our problems today stem from the fact we no longer have families who stay together and the children are either left to their own devices or feel unloved and betrayed. If every couple who married, all starry-eyed and expecting a "lived-happily-ever-after" existence, were committed to their vows, there would not be so many divorces. God ordained that a couple become "one", *forsaking all others*. Too many times this doesn't happen. Neither party seems ready to give up his/her "rights." Because the newly married couple is not ready to settle into a mature relationship, disaster befalls them when the trials and tribulations of parenthood hit them like a hurricane. I've heard that there are more children in school with only one parent than those with two. It's so true that the best gift any parent can give a child is to love the other parent, making a loving, cohesive family.

What "right" do any of us have? According to our Declaration of Independence that our forefathers signed on July 4, 1776, we read: *We hold these truths to be self-evident, that all men are created equal, that they are endowed by their Creator with certain unalienable rights, that among those are Life, Liberty and the Pursuit of Happiness.*

That means everyone has the *equal* right to life, liberty and the pursuit of happiness, not that all men are equal. Even those unalienable rights have been taken away. Every baby no longer has the "right" to be born. The government has ordained otherwise. Some people think "liberty" means they can do whatever they please, no matter how it affects others. An activity that makes one person "happy" is oftentimes either outright wrong or harmful to others.

As I see it, there is a solution to all the evil taking place. **Commit thy way unto the Lord; trust also in Him; and He shall bring it (the good) to pass.** (Psalm 37:5)

Commitment to What

When we think of people as being "committed" we usually mean they believe in what they are doing so much that they devote every waking minute to achieve their goal. This applies to all terrorists, I believe. They are so committed to their belief that they willingly give their lives to obtain that goal. That almost seems barbaric to those of us in the civilized world. But, is it?

Remember Daniel and his three friends from the Old Testament? As young Hebrews they refused to eat and drink the king's food and wine even though refusing meant death. They managed to convince their keeper that he should give them ten days to prove their point about what they should eat. If they were not better, they would then abide by the king's ruling. They proved to be right.

Later Daniel's three friends were threatened with being thrown into the fiery furnace unless they bowed down to the king's idol. I don't know about you, but I wonder how strong my faith would be at such a time. Again, the Lord God protected them and convinced the king that they did have a God worth serving. Would you trust God to protect you if you were thrown into a hungry lions' den?

Yes, the book of Daniel is full of miracles about how God protected the four young men who refused to bow to a king but instead followed their convictions and obeyed the True God. Daniel lived more than nine decades, advising kings and serving God for over 70 years.

Besides the terrorists today, we do have people in the modern-day world who refuse to give up their faith and are willing to suffer and even die to keep it. After Pastor Richard Wurmbrand, a Christian Jew, was beaten and tortured for 14 years (1948-1956) in a Rumanian prison, he made his way to the United States. Within three weeks of arriving here he testified before congress regarding the conditions under communist rule. He later organized *The Voice of Martyrs* which is still active today. Within the pages of their newsletter are numerous testimonies from people in third world countries who are standing up boldly for their belief in Jesus Christ and because of that, they have been beaten, tortured and killed.

There is one *huge difference* between a terrorist who is willing to die for his cause and a martyr. A terrorist will kill others as well as himself for what he believes; a martyr is willing to die but *never* takes another's life.

We here in America seem to lack that sort of commitment and perhaps that is why we see our country deteriorating. We Christians allow just a "little bit" of smut without speaking up. We read articles about the torturing and inhumane treatment of animals but say nothing about the destruction of human life when it comes to aborting babies. We read about men who have been sentenced to prison for taking the lives of two people, their wife and the baby in her womb, and still we condone abortion. What's wrong with that kind of logic? We allow pornography in entertainment of every kind because our constitution gives us the "right of free speech." Don't we realize that we also have the right to reject that swill? We don't have to support the books, magazines, songs, movies, etc. that spew such garbage. But, we obviously do since those who promote that appear to be prospering.

In a little over a year we will be electing new leaders for our country. Are we willing to study each person's character to make sure the leaders we get are true representatives of the moral fiber we would like to see make a comeback? It is way past time for Christians to make commitments that stand for God's way. What is God's way, you ask? He told the Israelites in II Chronicles 7:14. ***If my people, which are called by my name, shall humble themselves, and pray, and seek my face, and turn from their wicked ways; then will I hear from heaven, and will forgive their sin, and will heal their land.***

Counting My Blessings

Our Sunday school teacher asks, "What blessings have you had this week?" It isn't long until someone shares an event that caused him or her to be thankful. There have been times when we start by naming a blessing for every letter of the alphabet. When one lives in America, the land of the free and the home of the brave, it isn't too difficult to think of ways we have been blessed.

While listening to a missionary who was back on furlough from Nairobi, Kenya, I was reminded anew how very blessed we are! After telling about the destitute and total depravity of millions in a city that is modern in every way, someone asked, "Well, how do they buy food if there are no jobs? They have to eat!" The missionary raised his eyebrows and asked, "They do?" He went on to explain that having food to eat is not available to a great many who live on the streets. Given the choice of using 10 shillings to buy glue or bread, even homeless, small children will choose the glue. When they sniff that, they forget they are hungry. The bread will only satisfy for a short while.

The missionary's wife, a registered nurse, commented that hope for a better tomorrow is all they have. Once they come to believe in The Bread of Life, they have a new understanding of hope for the future. The missionaries assist them in helping themselves. That gave the recipients a sense of pride, of ownership.

In a Christmas message received from a pastor in Haiti, he stated what a blessing it was to just be alive! The reason he bothered to mention it at all is because death by starvation is an every day happening there. The same is true for many parts of the world. We see hunger here in America but it's not anywhere nearly as prevalent as it is in other countries. One meal a day of rice and beans is a blessing for many children and there's not even that much in some places of the world.

Americans have such an abundance of food it has caused us to suffer ill health. Our lifestyle in many ways keeps us from obeying the Lord, much less serving Him. If you have been blessed with good health, you have something money cannot buy...as many have discovered. Do you have two eyes, ears, hands, feet? Everyone doesn't but many of those who have been short-changed in that regard have more than made up for it with an attitude of choosing to do what they can with what they have. I watched a documentary about a 17-year-old high school girl who was born without arms, not even stubs. Yet, she was popular and as active as anyone with a fully developed body. She grew up accepting her situation and was blessed by parents who loved and accepted her.

Can anyone be blessed without friends? Not

I. Aside from the comfort God gives during a period of grieving the loss of a loved one, there is nothing to compare with knowing there are others who care for you and empathize with you.

Conversely, as the Bible says, ***Rejoice with them that rejoice.*** (Romans 12:15a) When a friend who had spent over six months near death's door stood up in front of the church at the close of the service to thank everyone for their prayers, there wasn't a dry eye in the house. The joy we all felt was more than our tear ducts could hold. Yes, friends add flavor to our lives that comes from nothing else.

If you are wealthy in a monetary way and using it for your own pleasure, you are missing blessings unimaginable. People who have used their worldly wealth to help others less fortunate have attested to that fact over and over, if they tell at all, that is.

We still have freedom in America to worship as we choose. Immigrants who were denied that privilege in their former homeland wonder why we are not more protective of our freedom and be concerned that we might lose it. While working on a program requiring signatures of registered voters, a lady with a definite accent offered, "I believe I must exercise my right to vote or keep my mouth shut if things don't go my way." If only more "home grown" Americans believed that, what a different country we might have today!

As I thought about the subject of "Blessings"

the words to *Count Your Blessings* kept running through my mind.

Count Your Blessings is generally considered to be the finest hymn ever written by Johnson Oatman, Jr. He lived from 1856 to 1922 and during his lifetime wrote words for over 5,000 gospel songs. Although he was a Methodist Episcopal minister, his full time work was in retail and insurance. In 1897 this hymn first appeared in *Songs for Young People*, a hymnal compiled and published by Edwin O. Excell, a contemporary of Oatman's. Since it was first introduced *Count Your Blessings* has been sung all over the world.

According to the information on the Internet, "Like a beam of sunlight it has brightened up the dark places of the earth. Perhaps no American was ever received with such enthusiasm in Great Britain as this hymn. *The London Daily*, in giving an account of a meeting presided over by Gypsy Smith, reported, Mr. Smith announced the hymn *Count Your Blessings* by saying, 'In South London the men sing it, the boys whistle it, and the women rock their babies to sleep on this hymn.'"

The words to the last verse of this beautiful hymn are especially appropriate for today. *So, amid the conflict, whether great or small, Do not be discouraged, God is over all; Count your many blessings, angels will attend, Help and comfort give you to your journey's end.* With the direction our world is taking, it is sometimes hard to think of blessings instead of problems and troubles. Just listening or reading the daily news can cause heartburn or ulcers if we let it.

For those of us who have children, there is no greater blessing than to have them embrace the Lord and live according to His precepts. Daily I count my blessings in this regard that, not only my son, but his wife and children also look to the Him for guidance.

One of my favorite passages in the Bible is Philippians, chapter 4. The entire chapter gives excellent advice and comfort on how to keep an upbeat mind and spirit in spite of what happens all around us. The apostle Paul writes in verses 8 and 9: ***Finally, brethren, whatsoever things are true, whatsoever things are honest, whatsoever things are just, whatsoever things are pure, whatsoever things are lovely, whatsoever things are of good report; if there be any virtue, and if there be any praise, think on these things. Those things, which ye have both learned, and received, and heard, and seen in me, do: and the God of peace shall be with you.***

Why not try starting with 'a' and name a blessing for all 26 letters of the alphabet? As for me, I'm counting my blessings, but, more than anything, I am thankful that I have a Heavenly Father, a Savior and a daily Guide. There are no better blessings ...anywhere!

Courage

The word 'courage' conjures up all sorts of scenes in my head. I think of an invalid who faces pain every day and still manages to smile. I see the pictures on TV of our fighting forces who stealthily make their way down the street of a far-away land, wondering if they will be killed by sniper fire. I wonder if a teenager is going to be able to withstand the prodding of a friend to "Try this, it'll make you feel good." How many times have we seen photos of children dying because of famine in their land? It takes a great deal of courage for all of them to face every day.

But, as a Christian, along another line, I ask myself, "Would I deny Christ as my Savior if a gun were pointed at my head?" In so many countries today that happens more than we like to think. In the publication *Voice of the Martyrs* there are stories after story of Christians who are tortured and put in prison because they refuse to deny Christ as Savior. The following is one man's testimony after he was released from his 11-year imprisonment because he preached the gospel.

"They would kick me in the back and punch me in the stomach. They would mock me and say, 'So you are the son of the King of kings, a royal subject from a royal family. How does this feel now? I nearly died...sent to the hospital. In prison I took every opportunity to spread the

gospel. I gave my life to Jesus in 1989, after listening to short wave radio. When police interrogated me, I would tell them, 'I am alive today by God's grace upon my life. I live for Jesus. I will not give up my Lord. If you kill me, I will be with Him. I knew my wife and others were praying. If I died in prison, they could do anything with my body, as I know where I am going. The Lord Jesus is always walking ahead of us and has preached a pathway for all of us to walk. I told the Christian prisoners who faced bouts of severe depression, 'Hold on to your faith, because even if they kill you, you will go to heaven and live forever.'" (*Voice of the Martyrs*, June 2006)

Some Christians have been tortured for having a Bible. Churches have been closed. A friend recently said to me, "You know, we are getting so bad in America, we need missionaries here as much as they are needed overseas." I don't know about that since we still have the opportunity and the privilege to read our Bible, to go to church and to share the Good News. In many parts of the world they have never heard the gospel at all. But those who have accepted Christ are willing to die for Him.

Courage? We are wimps in comparison to those suffering for Christ's sake around the world. A question I heard long ago comes to mind. Is there enough evidence in my life to convict me of being a Christian? With the way America is heading, I may some day have to answer that. I wonder, how courageous will I be? In Luke 12:8 & 9 Jesus said, **Whosoever shall confess me before men, him shall the Son of man also confess before the angels of God: But he that denieth me before men shall be denied before the angels of God.**

Courage, Not Fear

We are at a time in our history when there is fear in every aspect of our lives. War. Economy. Environment. Tragedies. It's little wonder people are turning off the news reports and not reading the newspapers. Enough already! Right? When is it going to end?

My heart aches for families who are separated because of the war and especially for those who have lost loved ones or have been maimed. I can understand why some are saying, "It's not worth it!" However, I am reminded of the men who fought to form "a more perfect union" over 232 years ago. Do they even teach about the Constitution and the Declaration of Independence in our schools now? With the Internet, a valuable source at times, it's easy to learn about any subject of interest.

It has been decades since I studied our nation's beginning history so I checked the Internet to refresh my memory. One thought struck me, it could not have been easy just traveling from Maine to Georgia to finalize the Declaration of Independence. Of the 13 colonies, there were nine men who were not born in America. They had left England, Ireland, Scotland and Wales, seeking a better life. Out of the 56 signers, some were lawyers (self-trained among them), teachers, physicians, farmers and merchants. They were the cross section of the country then. The youngest, Edward Rutledge, was only 26 years old while Benjamin Franklin was 70. Our second and third presidents, John Adams and Thomas Jefferson, were among the signers.

The actual document was first drafted in June and on July 2, 1776 was finalized (just as the British were arriving in New York) and presented July 4, 1776. It wasn't until August all signers had added their signatures. Congress, sitting in Baltimore, Maryland on January 18, 1777 ordered the signed copies of the document be sent to all the states.

Where is the courage today to fight for the freedom they gave their all to give us? They must have had the following scriptures in mind to be willing to risk dying for their beliefs.

So that we may boldly say, The Lord is my helper, and I will not fear what man shall do unto me. (Hebrews 13:6) ***The Lord is my light and my salvation; whom shall I fear? The Lord is the strength of my life; of whom shall I be afraid?*** (Psalm 27:1) And one of my favorite verses is found in the center of the whole Bible: ***It is better to trust in the Lord than to put confidence in man.*** (Psalm 118:8)

Discerning God's Will

Christ prayed in the Garden of Gethsemane before he was betrayed, **O my Father, if it be possible, let this cup pass from me: nevertheless not as I will, but as thou wilt.** (Matthew 26:39b) He knew what was to come and yet he was willing to obey God's will. He knew that, without the shedding of His blood, there could be no restoration between God and mankind.

If he was willing to obey God, though it required going through torture, humiliation and even death, shouldn't we? Therein lays the question, "How do I know what God wants for me?" That is where discernment enters the picture. Every day we have to make choices. Some are mundane, minor ones, such as, "What kind of bread do I want?" Others are serious assessments which may have lasting consequences on our lives. Anyone with an addiction conquers his/her problem one day at a time; sometimes one hour at a time.

I heard a sermon on prayer fasting. The minister told about how often God's people has fasted *and prayed* to change their situation. Most everyone realizes that alcoholism, drugs and sexual perversions are wrong but why is gluttony not considered sinful? The word 'discernment' means to judge with the eyes or your mind. People addicted to food oftentimes fail that test. I know because as I listened to the sermon I felt as if someone were stepping all over my toes.

Another area where we fail is when it comes to choosing a life partner. We either act on attraction only or we pray and ask God's leading to make the right choice. Many Christians have problems because we don't ask for God's help *first.*

The best source to train our thinking and our actions is found in the Holy Bible. In Hebrews 4:12 it states, **For the word of God is quick and powerful and sharper than any two-edged sword, piercing even to the dividing asunder of soul and spirit, and of the joints and marrow, and is a discerner of the thoughts and intents of the heart.**

It took me years to realize that we need to read our "guide book" if we want to grow in our spiritual life. Consequently, I learned the hard way just as others have, making one mistake after another. What a difference it makes when we follow God's rules! The apostle Paul wrote to the Philippians about the secret of having the peace of God. **Be careful for nothing; but in every thing by prayer and supplication with thanksgiving let your requests be made known unto God. And the peace of God, which passeth all understanding, shall keep your hearts and minds through Christ Jesus.** (Philippians 4:6-7)

Existing Without Power

You flip a switch and instantly the room is filled with light. You turn the key and the door opens. You turn the key in your car and hear a hum. What happens if there is no light? Or opening? Or hum? Some of us might panic, especially if it's the key that turns your car's engine. We take so many things for granted, barely giving thought to the significance of the little things in life. The unexpected is not supposed to happen. But, it does, many times. "Power" encompasses many meanings. Electrical and gas power are necessities if we are to have the type of civilization we enjoy. Perhaps that's why there is so much greed involving the commodities that make that kind of power possible.

Why do people spend millions of dollars to run for a public office that pays a pittance in comparison? Obviously, it is the power they hope to attain. This year we have already seen how much has been spent to achieve the goal of becoming the "most powerful person" on earth. There are those who don't care one way or another who wins and, if they vote, they either vote selfishly for what they perceive benefits them or vote however someone else tells them. How tragic that we who inherited a free nation after much bloodshed take our privilege so lightly.

Edmund Burke (1729-1797), an Irish philosopher who served in the House of Commons, was a promoter of our American Revolution. He said, *"The only thing necessary for evil to triumph is for good men to do nothing."* That's why despots come to power over nations...people do nothing. Those of us old enough to remember Hitler and Stalin can attest to the horrors then. Today we still have the same type of men in power in various countries around the world. That kind of power destroys.

In February three of our past presidents are remembered. All three made a difference during the time they served our country. Washington certainly proved to be a great leader as our nation was formed. Lincoln persevered to keep us one nation and Reagan helped destroy the hold communism had on the world. How did they do it? They were all strong Christians who believed in Almighty God and called upon Him and His strength and power for help.

That is exactly what is needed today.

In reading the story of Joseph in the book of Genesis, it's amazing how he gained so much power without trying. That's because God, who is *all powerful*, was directing the outcome. When Joseph told his parents and brothers about his dream that some day he would rule over them, his brothers decided to get rid of him. For thirteen years, Joseph was treated badly although he did nothing wrong. Then, through the visions God gave him, he became the most powerful man in Egypt except for Pharaoh.

Eventually, his long ago dream became a reality and his brothers came begging to him. Joseph realized that all the terrible things he had endured were God's preparation to save the nation of Israel. One of the most moving passages in the Bible is when Joseph reveals his true identity to his brothers who had sold him into slavery. ***I am Joseph, your brother, whom you sold into Egypt. Now therefore be not grieved nor angry with yourselves...for God did send me before you to preserve life. ...So now it was not you that sent me hither, but God.*** (Genesis 45:4b,5,8)

How many times in my life have I fretted and stewed and worried about something that never came to fruition? Too many because my human nature took control and that prevented me from seeking God's will in *all* things.

We need to remember Christ's last words as he ascended into heaven, ***All power is given unto me in heaven and in earth.*** (Matthew 28:18) He then sent the Holy Spirit to be our constant companion. We choose to have the added power or not. As the song by Mylon R. LeFevre states,

Without Him, I could do nothing,
Without him I'd surely fail;
Without Him I would be drifting
like a ship without a sail.
(© 1963 by The LeFevres)

The Holy Spirit is our generator and will give us all the power we need to accomplish what Christ wants us to do. Our job is to submit our will to him. Until we do, we are like the switch that doesn't turn the light on; or the key that doesn't unlock the door; or the engine that doesn't start our car and we, too, may end up going nowhere, accomplishing nothing for Christ.

Fear of What? Whom?

These days are filled with news of fear and/or terror. *Beware...keep your eyes open...be alert.* Ever since September 11, 2001, America has lived under a whole new set of rules and behavior. New laws aimed at protecting us from further destruction, so we're told. "Things" just ain't what they used to be! Furthermore, I doubt if they ever will be again.

Whose fault is it? The answer to that stirs up a lot of controversy...and, I mean a LOT! There are some who blindly obey whatever the authorities tell them to do or not to do. Others protest vehemently, believing their "rights" are being trampled on.

At the time of this writing, America is embroiled in another war. Most of the fierce fighting is over and there is not a doubt in my mind that we will eventually win. But, at what cost? Is helping out another country worth dividing our own?

When this country was first born, the Founding Fathers did not hesitate to make laws that would protect our freedom. It has been reported that all 56 signers of the Declaration of Independence died as paupers. There must have been a lot of fear in their minds as to the consequences of what they were doing, but in their hearts they knew they were right. We can all thank God for every one of them.

The book of Proverbs in the Bible is one of the

best teachers because of the wise instructions found therein. For instance, in the very first chapter, we read, **How does a man become wise? The first step is to trust and reverence the Lord! Only fools refuse to be taught**. (Proverbs 1:7)

In the Kings James version, the same verse states, **The fear of the Lord is the beginning of wisdom.** And, the same admonition is repeated later on. That does not refer to a fear of what God *will* do to us but rather an awesome kind of fear because of the power He has and His *capability* to do anything. As all the pros and cons regarding the present turmoil are discussed, I'm pleased when someone applies the wisdom of scripture to his/her thinking. Unfortunately, we do not all approach scripture with the same understanding. But, at least by applying it, as we understand it, we start.

As a child, my greatest fear was what happened to me when I disobeyed my parents. If I got in trouble at school, the last thing I wanted was to have my misdemeanor reported to my folks because I knew I would be in bigger trouble. Nowadays, it seems the teachers or schools get in trouble if they try to practice discipline in any form. The ones who fear now are the teachers. Not good as we have learned.

In spite of keeping the Bible and prayer out of the schools, TV has shown us that, when facing possible death, the fighting men and women do call on the protection of God. According to one report I heard, the worship services in the desert have been full. It would be wonderful if all Americans here on safer ground realized how important taking time for God is.

There are many kinds of fear besides terror that we face every day. Fear of losing our health or our finances is something many seniors face. Fear of losing a job is stressful for a good many as they watch their company downsize. Those are understandable fears to be sure. But, what is accomplished by worrying? Nothing. Nada. Zilch. The Bible gives us a better answer. ***Casting all your care upon him (Jesus); for he careth for you.*** (I Peter 5:7) Easy to read and say, but difficult to do. As one friend said, "I keep praying to God to help me, but then I take the burden back. It's as if I don't really believe he's capable."

At a seminar I was privileged to hear Joan Brock describe what it was like when she suddenly lost her eyesight within a three-week period. Without any warning whatever, she became blind with only slight peripheral vision left. She was 32 years old at the time with a husband and young daughter. They managed to adjust with their new lifestyle. Then, again without any forewarning, her husband developed a fast-growing cancer and died shortly thereafter. She was now 36 years old and her daughter was eight.

One of the ways she coped was to keep a diary, writing everything down on how she succeeded. She was fortunate to have family and friends help her, but it was through her own faith in God that kept her spirits high and accepting her situation once she faced reality. From her diary notes, she wrote a book, *More Than Meets The Eye,* which was made into a movie. Now, she is a writer and in demand as a speaker. With her keen sense of humor, she says, "Can you believe it...a woman getting paid to talk!" She ended her remarks with an acronym for HOPE.

H–(use your) <u>head</u>, (which leads to your) <u>heart</u>, (and) <u>heed</u> God's Word

O–<u>order</u> or <u>organization</u> (which gives us peace)

P–<u>pause</u> and <u>pray</u> (and we'll find a) <u>purpose</u> (which also brings) <u>peace</u>

E–<u>enlighten</u>; <u>encourage</u> (allows us to) <u>embrace</u> hope

I have yet to meet anyone who, at one time or another, has not been fearful of something. All sorts of phobias are built into our human nature. It's so easy to fear, but in all things, God has provided the answer for us.

Trust in the Lord with all thine heart; and lean not unto thine own understanding. In all they ways acknowledge him, and he shall direct they paths. (Proverbs 3:5, 6)

Finding Inner Peace

In a world such as we have today, can there be any *real* peace? Many years ago I took a class on hypnotism. (I discovered I could not be hypnotized.) In one of the exercises the instructor asked us to close our eyes and picture a peaceful scene in our minds. Immediately, I saw a quiet lake with beautiful surroundings of flora. A lot of men with busy, hectic lives oftentimes imagine the same scene except they are in a boat, hanging onto a fishing rod. Go to a mountaintop and gaze out upon God's creation. It's exhilarating to view the beauty our eyes behold and one senses utter peace.

Change of scenery. Watch the daily telecasts. It breaks my heart to see the evil that tears countries apart. I wonder how children who see such horrific scenes can ever get over them. Too many service men and women have returned from war, scarred for life because of the utter horror of what they have witnessed.

When war breaks out and the enemy is defeated, it doesn't always mean continuing peace has been attained. Certainly, that has been proven to be the case recently in Iraq where terrorists fight on because they fear freedom for their people. The Bible tells us that we will *never* have peace on earth. At least, not the kind where there are no wars in the world. From the beginning of mankind, there have been struggles for power.

That doesn't mean there can be no *inner peace* within one's self. In John's Gospel, he records Christ's words, **In the world you will have tribulation: but be of good cheer; I have overcome the world.** Earlier in chapter 14 of John's Gospel, we read the familiar phrase often quoted at funerals: **Peace I leave with you, my peace I give unto you: not as the world gives, give I unto you. Let not your heart be troubled, neither let it be afraid.**

Any realtor will tell you that the most important thing to remember when buying a house is "location, location, location." To have inner peace in this life, we might change that "L" word to "lifestyle, lifestyle, lifestyle." The reason is that much of the stress and frustration we suffer is due to poor choices we make.

How many hangovers have been caused from making poor choices the night before? How much sickness occurs because of smoking? Gluttony? Promiscuity? Arguments? Over spending? It has been said that stress is at the root of a lot of illnesses, such as high blood pressure, arthritis and even cancer. Why do we humans keep on making blunders instead of learning from the misdeeds of others? Because we're human.

According to Dr. D. James Kennedy, pastor of the Coral Ridge Hour on TV from Ft. Lauderdale, Florida, twenty-six times in history governments have been defeated because of the sexual sin and cultural breakdown of the people. One of the earliest such devastations we learn about happened to Sodom and Gomorrah in Genesis, chapter 19.

"The average age of the world's greatest civilizations from the beginning of history, has been about 200 years," wrote Alexander Tyler, a Scottish history professor at the University of Edinborough in 1787. During those years, nations progressed through the following sequence: "From bondage to spiritual faith; spiritual faith to great courage; courage to liberty; liberty to abundance; abundance to complacency; complacency to apathy; apathy to dependence; dependence back into bondage."

It is possible to have real peace in the home when Christ is at the helm and all family members look to Him for guidance and dependency. Paul gave excellent advice on how to accomplish that feat when he wrote the following to the Philippians 4:6,7, **Be careful for nothing; but in every thing by prayer and supplication with thanksgiving let your requests be made known unto God. And the peace of God, which passeth all understanding shall keep your hearts and minds through Christ Jesus.**

Follow Me

Actions *always* speak louder than words. "Do what I say, not what I do" is an admonition stated by more than one parent who has had a child mimic him/her. Unfortunately, it doesn't work that way in real life.

The Israelites were instructed to diligently teach their children **to love the Lord, thy God with all thine heart, and with all thy soul, and with all thy might.** (Deuteronomy 6:5) In Proverbs 22:6 we read **Train up a child in the way he should go; and when he is old, he will not depart from it.** Perhaps that's where recent generations have failed. It has been said by those who keep such data that the last two generations have not been exposed to, much less brought up in, the church. Parents have fallen by the wayside, neglecting any spiritual training of their children. Now, some of those offspring have become interested in finding solace for their troubled souls. A charismatic person comes along and draws them into the fold.

There are many large congregations today led by charismatic leaders. Last year the news exposed us to a church that had an extremely controversial pastor who preaches hate and anything but the true gospel and love of Christ. Yet, his church is packed every Sunday. Another preacher has gained infamous fame because of his hatred of homosexuals. There is no preaching of forgiveness or the love of Christ. Just hate. Then there's the renowned young preacher who never attended Bible college but has one of the largest congregations in the country. He "inherited" his position after his father died.

What a tragedy! A disciple is one who follows the teachings of another. The followers of those preachers are disciples, but not Christ's disciples. A Christian disciple is one who follows the teachings of Christ which include, besides love and salvation, mercy and forgiveness.

In a devotional the question was asked, How can you tell the "real" one dollar bill? There were three choices: a) study counterfeit money, b) study the differences between counterfeit and real money, c) study real money. The answer was "c" The same can be said about true religion. What better place to learn about the One True God than from His holy inspired Word, the Bible?

A relative once told me he didn't go to church because there were too many hypocrites there. It's true, when someone professes Christianity but whose life doesn't show it, that person is a hypocrite. But, since no human is perfect, we are not to pattern our lives after *any person*...only Christ. That's because He's the only Perfect One. The rest of us are either saved sinners or unsaved sinners. As the beautiful hymn says, *Turn Your Eyes Upon Jesus.* If we do that, we will have a perfect teacher to follow.

Growing Up

It's interesting that the Bible reveals very little about Christ's growing up years. We read he taught his elders in the temple when he was 12 years old and the next reference to his age is 30. Most of us who have passed through the teen years know they can be difficult...*very* difficult; not only for the teen but for the parents. Since we are told that Christ was perfect...and I accept that...it would have been nice to have some actual teaching as to how he handled various situations. Instead we are given a brief verse in Luke 2:52 which states: **Jesus kept increasing in wisdom and stature, and in favor with God and men**. We know from that last phrase he was exemplary as he matured.

For those of us who were anything but exemplary teenagers, challenging our parents every step of the way toward our maturity, it's hard to realize how someone could be so good. More than one comedian has quipped that, "If you haven't matured by age 50, it's too late." I disagree. Some of us finally decide that life is much easier when we abide by the Biblical teachings rather then doing things "our way." With that decision, we begin to mature, no matter how long it takes or how old we are.

Joseph, who was sold into slavery by his jealous brothers, is another Bible character I admire. Without committing any sin, he fell into hard times because of his brothers' treatment and then lying by Pharaoh's wife. Later, when he forgave his brothers because he realized all that happened had been according to God's plan, we see a picture of Christ who stands ready to forgive us of all our sins.

Because of the technology today, young people are exposed to every sort of sin and corruption known to man. It is a different world from the one I experienced while growing up. However, we have a promise that **Jesus Christ is the same yesterday and today and forever**. (Hebrews 13:8) No matter how we are tempted, He is our surefire safeguard to lead us down the strait and narrow path on our way to full-blown maturity. If we need help, James gave us the answer to that when he wrote, **But if any of you lacks wisdom, let him ask of God, who gives to all men generously and without reproach, and it will be given to you**. (James 1:8)

In other words, there's no excuse for anyone not to mature *if* he/she has that desire. Help is just a prayer away.

Have and Have Not

At the end of August 2005, America watched in horror as one of its largest cities was devastated. How could something like that happen here in America? At this writing the "blame game" has begun and it will probably be a long time before there are solutions or answers to what really happened. Not only did an act of nature destroy the city but some of its residents committed all sorts of criminal acts in the aftermath.

Seeing such sights was not a first for me. Over the years I've watched missionary films from Third World countries that tell of unimaginable poverty to those of us who live in this land of the free and home of the brave. Abandoned children...very young children... trying to eke out a living on the streets, eating anything they can get their hands on and prostituting their bodies in order to exist.

But, to watch people behave as animals gone wild here in this country was sickening. Many of those people had nothing to lose to begin with. Is that why they went berserk when they had the opportunity to satiate their desires?

My heart ached for those who lost everything they had. How would I feel? Could I come away just thankful to be alive as many of them stated they were?

There once was a man a long time ago who

was said to be the richest man in the world at that time. The devil was given power to destroy all of his possessions. The only power the devil didn't have was over his life. God retained that power. What the devil did to Job is well known to anyone who ever attended Sunday school. He lost everything he owned, including his ten children, and his body was attacked. The only one left in his family was his wife who, it turned out, wasn't a very good supporter. In fact, she said to him, **Dost thou still retain thine integrity? curse God and die!** (Job 2:9)

As three friends came to visit with him, each trying to convince him he had been guilty of some sin and needed to ask God for forgiveness, Job remained steadfast. He affirmed, **I know that my redeemer liveth and that he shall stand at the latter day upon the earth.** (Job 19:25)

Finally, a young man came to speak to him. He had waited until the elders had finished with their opinions as to why Job was suffering. But, his words didn't solve Job's problem either. It was only after Job listened to God Himself tell how he was the only one who can control nature, the beasts of the earth and humans.

Once Job realized this and bowed his will to God, then prayed for his misguided friends, God blessed him with twice his previous wealth and gave him another ten children.

On September 11, 2001 we watched in unbelieving horror the tragedy here in America when terrorists hit New York, Washington, D.C. and Pennsylvania. All at once, *all* Americans felt as if they had personally been attacked. God's wrath didn't cause that ravage act. It was deliberate evil; an evil that had been growing for decades but ignored. Americans proved their fortitude and quickly combined efforts to heal the wounds.

With Hurricane Katrina, we witnessed valor and uncanny bravery but at the same time reactions by some never before seen in America. So, where do we find the hope to rebuild? The answer lies in a hymn written by Edward Mote, entitled *The Solid Rock*.

> *My hope is built on nothing less*
> *Than Jesus' blood and righteousness;*
> *I dare not trust the sweetest frame,*
> *But wholly lean on Jesus' name.*
>
> *On Christ the solid rock I stand.*
> *All other ground is sinking sand.*
> *All other ground is sinking sand.*

If America is to be healed of whatever caused the insidious actions of some and become the prosperous nation we once were, it's not possessions we need. We need God back in our lives to guide and direct us just as our Founding Fathers called upon Him at the birth of our nation.

He Restoreth My Soul

Of all the promises God gave us, one of my favorites is found amid the well known 23 Psalm. **He restoreth my soul.** When we reach the limit of what we can take, God has promised to renew our strength, to lift us up and to restore our disheartened soul.

Restoration of anything is good. Restoring a friendship after a misunderstanding is heartwarming. Restoring old homes has become an avocation for some. I remember how my grandfather used to restore furniture after he retired. He had learned the trade as a young boy when he worked with his grandfather. I can still hear him explain, "You have to tie each spring eight times" as he repaired a sunken seat of a chair before recovering it.

Any gardener will tell you pruning is an important part of upkeep. When I pruned a large plant in my home before it pushed its way through the ceiling, I took a saw and cut off the top half of the two stalks. It rested for a short time before springing forth with six...not two...new growths that are now on their way to the ceiling.

God does the same with us. Those who have gone through hard times learn that they are better for the experience. They are stronger, more compassionate and have an understanding lacking before. Very few people in this country or the world do not know who Billy Graham is.

In spite of his preaching and teachings his own son and a grandson strayed far away from God. After living the life of prodigal sons, both have been restored to fulltime Christian ministries. As someone has said, "Every believer is a witness for Christ whether he wants to be or not." In other words, sometimes we are the only Bible others read. Calling oneself a Christian and acting like the devil is like taking the Lord's name in vain.

In Psalm 51 King David admits his sin with Bathsheba. The whole chapter is a plea to God to forgive him. In verses 12 and 13 we read: ***Restore unto me the joy of thy salvation; and uphold me with thy free spirit. Then will I teach transgressors thy ways; and sinners shall be converted unto thee.***

In my mind America has reached such a low point I wonder how much more God will put up with before making us pay for our sins unless we repent. Our culture is one of "anything goes" until there's nothing sacred left.

Teachers fear for their lives and students openly call them vulgar names without fear of a reprimand.

Criminals are either slapped on the wrist and told, "Naughty, naughty" before being turned loose, given suspended sentences, or very little time in prison.

Our congress is made up of men and women who are routinely caught misbehaving but because they are elected officials, too often they are not held responsible for their actions.

When the government does try to help with such things as Medicare and Medicaid, there's so much corruption among the participants, it becomes too expensive.

Even the religious community has suffered because of the acts of a few clergy.

The entertainment world seems to be hell personified. Who is there left for our young people to admire? Although there are some good examples one has to look long and hard to find them because the rotten apples get so much attention.

Restoration? Yes, we all need it as a daily process and with King David we should pray, **Create in me a clean heart, O God; and renew a right spirit within me** since we are all sinners in need of God's Grace. Through the prophet Micah, God tells his people, **I will take vengeance in anger and wrath upon the nations that have not obeyed me.** (Micah 5:15)

If Only…

Ask politicians what they want to be remembered for and you'll hear a litany of their accomplishments and the legacy they worked so hard to achieve. We are no different. *If only* we had listened to our parents, maybe we wouldn't have got into trouble. *If only* we had studied harder and worked for better grades, we'd have a better education. *If only* we had more money, we wouldn't have to scrape so much. *If only* we took better care of our bodies, we would have better health. The *if only* list is endless.

In Deuteronomy 28 God tells the Israelites to obey or else. In the New Testament John records Christ's words of instructions in the 15th chapter of his gospel wherein Christ reiterates the same message from the Old Testament. **If a man remains in me…he will bear much fruit. If anyone does not remain in me, he is like a branch that is thrown away and withers. If you remain in me …ask whatever you wish and it will be given you.** Throughout the chapter the word "*if*" is used a total of eleven times, giving promises for obeying and warnings if we don't.

A monthly newsletter from Sudan African Mission related they now have 300,000 converts. It's amazing because this mission was started by a retired pastor who knew about mechanical operations and was sent to Sudan as an instructor to teach the natives how to repair hospital equipment. He befriended one man whom he led to Christ. From that one man, the Sudan African Mission was born and today includes a medical facility, a Bible college and a potential of 3600 churches! When asked by skeptics in America about the truth of the numbers, Paul Douglass said, "When you have 20 ordained, sold out Evangelists going out from your church crying on every street then you will have 1000's to report also." The Douglasses started their ministry in Sudan in 1988 and are still going strong in their 80s. That's quite a legacy with that many fruitful "Timothys" to their credit.

Every one of us wants to believe that our life has meaning to others in some way. It is human nature. Perhaps we'd all have a better legacy *if* we obeyed God. *If* we did, rather than satiating ourselves with our own desires, we could leave a legacy so that when we meet our Lord face to face he will welcome us with, **Well done, thou good and faithful servant. You have been faithful with a few things; I will put you in charge of many things. Come and share your Master's happiness.** (Matthew 25:21)

Importance of Resurrection

New car styles today remind me of some when I was a child decades ago. The same goes for clothing and hair styles. The preacher in Ecclesiastes wrote, **What has been will be again, what has been done will be done again; there is nothing new under the sun.** (Chapter 1:9). "But," you ask, "what about all the new technology? We're now able to reach other planets."

True and I'll be the first to admit that most of the new technology is far beyond my comprehension. But then, so is much of the ancient architecture. How were some of the centuries-old castles and cathedrals, with their sky-reaching spires, built without modern tools and equipment? As I look at pictures of Dubai's new tallest structure in the world, I think of the Tower of Babel. God intervened then and the more we think we have the knowledge and capability to do anything our minds conceive I wonder if God might intercept man's accomplishments again. If we study past civilizations, it seems there was a cutting off period when they disappeared. Why? By whom? Could it be that any "new" creation of man is something that has always been and God Almighty has allowed man to "discover" it in HIS time?

But, what about the spiritual realm? The

Bible tells us that anyone who accepts Christ can be a ***new creature in Christ***. (2 Corinthians 5:17) That means we have been elevated to include a new spiritual life. Our old self should no longer be in control. The blessing is that *when* we fail (and we all do), we have a way of being forgiven. ***If we confess our sins he is faithful and just and will forgive us our sins and purify us from all unrighteousness.*** (I John 1:9) When our time on earth is up, we will be resurrected with a new spiritual eternal body if we remain faithful until the end.

We have hope and assurance when we read Paul's words in I Corinthians 15:3-6. ***Christ died for our sins according to the Scriptures, that he was buried, that he was raised on the third day according to the Scriptures, and that he appeared to Peter, and then to the Twelve. After that, he appeared to more than 500 hundred of the brothers at the same time.*** He is the only Living God because He defeated death. Robert Lowry wrote:

Up from the grave He arose,
With a mighty triumph o'er His foes;
He arose a Victor from the dark domain,
And He lives forever with His saints to reign.
He arose! He arose! Hallelujah! Christ arose!"

Non-Transferable

"You're going to church tomorrow, I presume," said my friend who had long since stopped the practice.

"Sure am. Why?" I asked.

"Just want you to cover for me," she joked.

"Sorry, it doesn't work that way. God doesn't have any grandchildren, in-laws or out-laws. That's something you have to do on your own 'cause it's an individual matter." That's not to say we can't pray for others. In fact, we should pray for them just as Jesus prayed for the lost in John 17.

Tony Fontaine was a singer who rejected his devout Christian parents' teachings to go out to make a name for himself. After nearly being killed in an auto accident and while comatose, he heard the doctors tell his wife that there wasn't much hope. He prayed to God that, if he could live, he would use his talents from then on to sing the Lord's praises. He fully recovered and kept his promise. Although, as an entertainer, much of his performances were in nightclubs, he always included a testimonial song in his repertoire. And, his own life was changed in that he no longer participated in the frivolity of nightclub living. He became a new man, using his talents to reach people on their turf.

When salvation is free, why is it that so many

people don't accept it? While vacuuming one Monday morning, I was reflecting on what the minister had said about reaching out and sharing the Good News with our neighbors. I thought of my young friend up the block, turned the vacuum off and proceeded to her house. I wanted to share this with her. She listened closely to what I told her and then responded, "When I get old like you, I'll think about it." I was probably 45 years old at the time.

Now is the day of salvation we read in II Corinthians 6:2. Some people are not given 70 years to think about it. Our time here on earth is but a *vapor* while eternity is unending. Is anything here on earth worth replacing for an unending heavenly bliss?

There are some that say there is neither a hell nor a God. The Bible calls such people fools. **The fool has said in his heart there is no God,** according to Psalm 14:1. For those who do believe in the Bible, we must take to heart the inspired words. The Bible tells us that God gave us a way to escape eternal damnation by accepting His Gift, Jesus Christ. In Hebrews 2:3 we read, **How shall we escape, if we neglect so great salvation; which at the first began to be spoken by the Lord, and was confirmed unto us by them that heard him?**

Pity the person who thinks one must become a "better" person before accepting Christ as Savior. In every Billy Graham crusade, the altar call is given as the choir sings *Just As I Am.* If you've listened to the words of the song, you'll understand why that song is chosen. Charlotte Elliott, who penned the words, was visiting friends when a minister mentioned he hoped she was a Christian. She was offended and told him she preferred not to discuss the subject. He answered that he always tried to speak a word for his Master and hoped she would too one day.

Only three weeks later, they met again and this time she asked him how she could come to know Christ. His reply was, "Just come as you are." She did and shortly after wrote the words to the hymn that's been around since 1865.

Becoming a Christian is not hard. The hard part is living a Christian life because all of us are human and prone to straying. We must be willing to obey Christ's commands. Like the apostle Paul who wrote to the Romans, **I do not understand what I do. For what I want to do I do not do, but what I hate I do**. (Romans 7:15 NIV) Christ knew that; therefore, He sent His Holy Spirit to guide and direct our daily steps. In spite of that, I've never met a perfect person and I don't expect to meet one while here on earth. I've been fortunate in meeting some saintly people, but no perfect ones. That's because there was only One Perfect Person who ever lived. Only Jesus Christ was qualified to take away our sins. **Neither is there salvation in any other: for there is none other name under heaven given among men, whereby we must be saved.** (Acts 4:12)

One of Those Days

It was April 2003, and one of *those* days. I was glued to the TV, listening to the saddest of news stories about the young pregnant woman and her infant's bodies being found and my heart ached for her family.

Then, I watched the joy and anticipation of the homecoming of the POWs from Iraq. How happy they were! What a great crowd awaiting their arrival! As one of them spoke later, he said he was remembering his fallen comrades who would never come home and he admonished us to remember and pray for their families.

My emotions were on a roller coaster ride...sad, thrilled, sad...total despair to exhilaration beyond limits. As my feelings went to the mountain top and back into the valley, I remembered that verse from the Bible, **Rejoice with them that do rejoice, and weep with them that weep** (Romans 12:15) and realized the Lord understood we would have such times. Just then the phone rang.

"Hi, Willa, this is Bonnie." At once my heart skipped a beat. My daughter-in-law usually does not initiate phone calls from them. My son normally comes on the line first.

"I thought I should let you know we had to take Steve to emergency today."

"What happened?" I gasped.

"Well, we're not sure and neither is the doctor yet, but Steve woke up with severe pain early this morning. He took a pain pill and that relieved him somewhat but not a great deal and after a few hours, he asked me to take him to the hospital. The worst part is we couldn't stay with him because of the SARS (severe acute respiratory syndrome) up here." They lived outside Toronto, Ontario at the time.

There went my emotional roller coaster again only this time it was personal. Other scriptures came to mind, **Casting all your care upon him; for he careth for you**, (I Peter 5:7) and **Pray without ceasing. In every thing give thanks: for this is the will of God in Christ Jesus concerning you**. (I Thessalonians 5:17, 18) I had my answer. After all, there is no one who fully understands our feelings and emotions better than the One Who made us.

Immediately after Bonnie's phone call, I went to my computer and sent out a prayer request, emailing nearly everyone on my list. I then phoned the lady at church who handles the prayer chain and sat down to offer my own prayers on my son's behalf. He was now in God's hands. I had done all I could. I was willing to put Steve in God's hands and willing to accept whatever the outcome might be, but I continued to pray all would turn out well.

During the night I awoke and decided I'd go

on the Internet and try to find out the hospital number. At the time Bonnie called, she said she didn't have a way of contacting Steve but would let me know as soon as she did. When I found the number, I called but since I didn't have an extension to dial, I could only listen to the instructions. When I heard all the information about how they were dealing with the SARS problem there, I became a little more concerned for anyone who had to be a patient in that environment.

By morning Bonnie called to give me the extension and I called Steve direct. He sounded much better and I was relieved and thankful. The doctors still weren't sure what had caused such severe pain but it may have been due to kidney stones. He has had them before but never to the extent this pain caused.

At church on that Easter morning, I could rejoice with everyone else. Then, our minister gave us the sad news that the six-year-old girl in our congregation who had been battling a rare cancer probably was not going to get well after all, according to what the doctors told her parents a couple of days before. We were stunned and extremely sad for her family.

But, this was Resurrection Sunday and once again the thought came to me that only God can relate to every emotion we face in our short lives. Therefore, we could rejoice *Because He Lives* and **God shall wipe away all tears from their** *eyes; and there shall be no more death, neither sorrow, nor crying, neither shall there be any more pain: for the former things are passed away.* (Revelation 21:4)

Hallelujah, what a Savior!

Praise the Lord!

Praise God, from Whom all blessings flow; Praise Him, all creatures here below; Praise Him above, ye heavenly hosts; Praise Father, Son and Holy Ghost. Amen. Every Sunday during my childhood after the offering, we stood and loudly proclaimed the Doxology, dragging out the "Amen". I became curious about this beloved hymn seldom sung in churches today.

The music was written by Louis Bourgeois in the 1500s and became known as "The Hundreth" after words based on Psalm 100 were added. We know that hymn as *All People That On Earth Do Dwell.*

Thomas Ken, an Englishman, (1637-1711) wrote the words to what we know as the Doxology, based on the words in Psalm 86:12. It has been said that those four lines of the hymn have been sung more frequently than any other song in all churches since then. In fact, it is believed those words teach the doctrine of the Trinity better than all the theological books written.

Think about them. *Praise God, from whom ALL BLESSINGS flow.* Can that be right? ALL blessings! Yes, I believe it's true. **Every good gift and every perfect gift is from above, and cometh down from the Father of lights, with whom is no variableness, neither shadow of turning.** (James 1:17) Even those things which cause us heartache and sadness usually occur because of their misuse. A gun, a knife, a car have all been instruments of death but it is the individual misusing them; not the item itself.

Praise Him, ALL CREATURES here below. That means you and me and every person alive. The animals among us seem to have an innate sense and in their way obey their Creator.

Praise Him above, ye heavenly hosts. At Christmastime, probably more than any other, we think of choirs of angels, proclaiming the birth of the Christ Child. Yet, in Hebrews 1:14 we read, **Are they** (speaking of angels) **not all ministering spirits, sent forth to minister for them who shall be heirs of salvation?** Those heavenly hosts are with us today, guiding and protecting us and still singing praises to God.

Praise FATHER, SON, and HOLY GHOST. There is it...the complete Godhead, Three-In-One, Triune Being.

It's true that the praise hymns we sing today are powerful and thrilling because many are taken directly from scripture. But, to me, the simple four lines written over 400 years ago can't be matched for the majesty they convey. I'd like to hear them more often.

Rebirth Gratitude

Sometime ago an imaginary story came through in an email, telling about an event in heaven. A new arrival was being shown around and coming to various rooms saw a lot of activity. The guiding angel explained that each room was busy fulfilling petitions sent to God. One room was receiving the requests and then separating them. Each room bustled with activity as the various pleas for health, finances, jobs, family matters, etc. were answered. Finally they arrived at a room where only one angel waited to have something to do. "Why is this angel not busy?" The response was, "This is the Gratitude Room and the truth is we don't get many replies."

In Luke 17 a story relates how Jesus healed ten lepers but only one returned to thank him...and he was a foreigner, a Samaritan! Too many times people are taken for granted. Often donors are not thanked because the recipients are too busy. Just as God gives and we take the blessings, we humans treat others the same way.

The Greatest Gift ever given was God's Only Begotten Son. Once we accept such a gracious gift, do we think, "Wow! Now I'm safe!" Or, do we actually reverse our sinful ways and, with the help of the Holy Spirit, follow a new , straighter path? ***Therefore, if anyone is in Christ, he is a new creation; the old has gone, the new has come! All this is from God, who reconciled us to himself through Christ and gave us the ministry of reconciliation: that God was reconciling the world to himself in Christ, not counting men's sins against them.*** (2 Corinthians 5:17-19) Just think, we can start anew with a clean slate!

Most people know that swearing by taking the Lord's name is wrong. The third commandment Moses received states, ***You shall not misuse the name of the Lord your God, for the Lord will not hold anyone guiltless who misuses his name.*** (Exodus 20:7) If we refer to ourselves as being a Christian, don't we have the responsibility to pattern our lives after Christ?

Another email story told about a policeman who arrested a woman after seeing her curse at other drivers and giving them unsavory signs. At the police station she proved the car was hers and he apologized. He then explained that he thought it was stolen because of the Christian bumper stickers and the "fish" emblem and he didn't think her actions matched those signs.

The world is watching and though no one is perfect, a Christian has an obligation to honor Christ in action and word. In this way, we show our gratitude for the rebirth we've been given.

Reconcile to Whom or What?

Wouldn't it be nice to live in a perfect place where there was never any sadness, or bad things happening? I've watched the Walgreen Drug Store commercial on TV, depicting just such an environment. Absolutely no problems whatever. But, they end with the truth that it's not for real because there is no perfect place anywhere to be found. At least, not today.

At one time there was. We know it as the Garden of Eden. When God created the earth and all that is in it, everything was perfect...the people, the animals, the climate...everything! But, he created man with the ability to choose because He didn't want robots worshiping Him. He wanted thinking persons to worship Him. Alas, there went the 'perfectness' of the Garden of Eden. I've heard all the jokes about how it was Eve's fault because she enticed Adam to eat the forbidden fruit. Since that fateful day, there has been imperfection in the world. Man became separated from God because he disobeyed one little law.

When I think about reconciliation, I ponder on all the different ways there are of being 'unreconciled' to coin a word. Every month when I sit down to reconcile what my checkbook says with what the bank tells me I have, I wonder if the figures will come out agreeing. When they do, I always whisper, "Thank you, Lord" because

I believe He's helped me keep my figures correct over the month.

A relative of mine seldom carries a checkbook with her. She uses counter checks that are handy in their small town. I asked her, "How do you know what your balance is?" "I just wait until I get the bank statement and then I know." That didn't make sense to me but then, a lot of people are living their lives the same way. They say they don't know if there is a heaven or a hell and are willing to wait until they die before finding out.

A friend told me once she always knew she had more money in her account than what was indicated on her check ledger because every time she turned to a new page, she rounded up the balance amount. I asked, "How do you reconcile with your bank statement then?" "Oh, I don't even try. I just take their word for what they say I have." That's an exercise in faith I can't afford since I need to keep track of my expenses. It is the kind of faith many Christians have, however. God has told us in His Word what He will do. They believe it and don't worry about it anymore. Their cares are in His hands.

Within families there have been many a heartache caused by something said in haste or anger. Sometimes the wound festers until it's nigh on impossible to be healed. This happened in my own family many years ago. I wrote something in anger and my brother refused to speak to me or attend any family gatherings for four years! My parents were hurt most by the standoff. There came a day, however, when he became a father and I asked if I could go see the baby. Permission was granted but he was nowhere around. However, a short time later when we both realized how ridiculous we had been, we "slid" into reconciliation that lasts to this day. Reconciling differences is difficult but not impossible if we admit fault, repent and ask forgiveness. Perseverance and determination are virtues. Stubbornness is not.

Our omnipotent God realized before He created man that he would fall. That's why He made plans for reconciliation even before He made the world. Mel Gibson's movie, *The Passion of the Christ*, reveals God's plan in a most vivid manner. We are shown in morbid detail the suffering and torture Christ endured when He took upon Himself the sins of the world. This was the only way man could be reunited with God for Christ Himself said**, God so loved the world that He gave His only Begotten Son, that whosoever believeth in Him should not perish but have everlasting life. For God sent not His Son into the world to condemn the world; but that the world through Him might be saved.** (John 3:16,17)

Every December, we joyfully celebrate the birth of Christ, the Babe in a manger. All the wonderful stories and songs fill our hearts with gladness. There is a hope for real peace! We will never see another Garden of Eden here on earth but for all believers in Christ, we cling to the promise that everlasting life in heaven will be more wonderful than anything we could imagine with our finite minds.

Renewal of the Mind

It has been said that it takes 21 days, three weeks, to establish a new habit...or drop an old one. Whatever we did before has to be abandoned and new thoughts and actions replace the gap. Evidently, there are people who have tried the theory and discovered it works. The trouble is it's hard to keep up a routine for 21 days.

My experience has been with dieting. The first week goes by like a strong wind with lots of gung-ho energy and enthusiasm. The second week is more like a gentle breeze; still eager for success but with less gusto for the idea. By the third week...well, it was a good idea but...and the excuses take over.

The same applies to any bad habit one has. Want to stop smoking? Drinking? Shopping? Drug use? Sexual perversion? It can be done with perseverance. We have to be willing to change our course; to give up what it is that's destroying us. Fortunately, there is help.

The Apostle Paul wrote in Romans 12:1-2: ***Therefore, I urge you, brothers, in view of God's mercy, to offer your bodies as living sacrifices, holy and pleasing to God – this is your spiritual act of worship. Do not conform any longer to the pattern of this world, but be transformed by the renewing of*** *your mind. Then you will be able to test and approve what God's will is – his good, pleasing and perfect will.*

In Psalm 51:10 King David cried out to God for mercy after he was made aware of his transgressions with Bathsheba. **Create in me a pure heart, O God, and renew a steadfast spirit within me.**

Perhaps our sins haven't included adultery or murder, but we all sin in some way every day. Unfortunately, the Bible doesn't distinguish between a "little" sin and a "big" one. Sin is sin...period!

The word picture Isaiah paints for us in Isaiah 40:31 is one everyone can obtain. **Those who hope in the Lord will renew their strength. They will soar on wings like eagles; they will run and not grow weary, they will walk and not be faint.**

With God's help, anything is possible...even a change in our habits. We first have to have a *renewal of the mind.*

Reward? Yes or No

At a political luncheon the speaker's subject was *What Is Your Legacy?* She spent a few minutes talking about how kids today are perceived to not be interested in history, that they simply want whatever they can get without any strings attached. Sort of an attitude that "Yesterday isn't my concern." She said that most kids would rather receive life's lessons from their parents but, "The fact is that parents have fallen down on their part."

If every parent would ask, *What is my legacy to my kids?* the results might be different. She reminded us that sometimes we're "too busy," or we don't realize that everything we do leaves some kind of a legacy. We need to lead (or teach) by example... and not by that age-old saying, *Do what I say, not what I do.* We need to encourage and inspire. She ended with the question, *Are you happy with your legacy?*

She certainly gave us much to think about. Since many of us are beyond the years of raising children we might be tempted to think it's too late for us to make a difference. But, is it? As I listened to the political speech, my mind wandered toward our spiritual legacy. Will we be greeted by our Lord with **thou good and faithful servant** (Matthew 25:21) or **I never knew you?** (Matthew 7:23) As long as we have breath whatever we do either adds or detracts from our spiritual legacy.

So, how do we build a legacy with God? One morning I woke up and my TV wouldn't work although it was fine the night before. After crawling around trying to find a loose connection, I pulled and reconnected one little plug and voilá, everything worked again. The experience made me think of how little God asks of us to be connected to Him. And, if we aren't connected to Him, how can we have a spiritual legacy? How can we expect a reward after our time on earth is up?

A sermon by a visiting preacher related how a huge redwood tree, hundreds of years old that started as a seedling, one day toppled to the ground. After a thorough investigation, it was discovered the foot traffic by admirers around the tree had damaged the root system. The minister linked how we humans need to be connected to God's root system, the Holy Bible. That's where we learn how to live and how to be sustained for all our trials.

A favorite scripture is, **I can do all things through Christ who strengthens me.** (Philippians 4:13) If we accept Christ as our Savior and the Bible as our guide, we will not only have eternal rewards, but will leave a good legacy for future generations.

Righteous? Yes, but...

The apostle Paul confessed that ***...the good that I would I do not: but the evil which I would not, that I do.*** (Romans 7:19) Beginning with verse 15, he struggles with our two natures...the good and the bad. He ends the chapter with, ***I thank God through Jesus Christ our Lord. So then with the mind I myself serve the law or God; but with the flesh the law of sin.*** As long as we remain here on earth, we will all give in to the law of sin from time to time. That is why we must *daily* ask God to cleanse us from sin.

We've all heard people use the excuse for not going to church because there are too many self-righteous hypocrites who attend. That's no doubt true. But, other people are not who we're supposed to follow. Christ said, **Follow me and I will make you fishers of men.** (Matthew 4:19) There is a hymn entitled *Turn Your Eyes Upon Jesus*. The chorus gives us our instructions.

Turn your eyes upon Jesus,
Look full in His wonderful face,
And the things of earth will grow strangely dim, In the light of His glory and grace.

Christ Himself is our Guide...not *any* man or woman because we are all flawed. On Judgment Day we will not be judged by what any other person does or doesn't do. We are responsible for our actions as everyone else is responsible for theirs. On the other hand, if we call ourselves a Christian, shouldn't we do all we can to follow Christ's examples and teachings? Isn't that what being a Christian means...a follower of Christ? Unfortunately, sometime those of us who claim Christ as his/her Savior are the only Bible others read. Someone asked, "Would you be convicted of being a Christian by your actions?" Would we? Could we?

It's scary to realize that because one is older and a longtime Christian, he/she is thought to be more righteous. Wrong! Unless a person actually reads the Bible, it is impossible to grow in the Christian faith. Years ago it was common to award a certificate to someone who never missed Sunday school. However, being present in the body didn't necessarily mean that person was present spiritually.

As a child I was forced to attend Sunday school and church. The one good development that accomplished was that it instilled in me a desire in adulthood to keep that habit. Truthfully, I was not always happy about attending. One time is vivid in my memory. I faked sickness to keep from going. Although I was miraculously "well" by the time the family returned home and ready to go play, my mother said, "No. If you were sick this morning, you'll stay inside all day to be sure you're OK." I never did that again! Thankfully, my parents set the right guidelines, following the scripture that says, **_Train up a child in the way he should go; and when he is old, he will not depart from it._** (Proverbs 22:6)

Being righteous is a goal to strive for while making sure we don't become self-righteous. Keeping our eyes on the Lord is the *only* way to achieve that.

The Best Is Yet To Come

I attended two funerals for dear friends in one week. Some have said, "When you get to be our age, you gotta expect those things to happen." In each case, these friends were younger than I. However, they were released from the pain and suffering they had endured for years. Their services were celebrations of a better life for them, one so beautiful words cannot describe it in human terms.

The Apostle Paul wrote, **If in this life only we have hope in Christ, we are of all men most miserable**. (I Corinthians 15:19) It's true...our hope lies in going from the imperfect now to attaining the perfect world of eternity with Christ.

A story has made the rounds on email about the lady who always kept her fork at a potluck because, "The best is yet to come," referring to the dessert. Then the correlation was made that, to all Christians, "The best *is* yet to come" because we believe in a world where there is no pain, no suffering, no sickness, no tears and *no death*! Such a belief gives us a hope that goes beyond human understanding.

To be sure, we Christians can become discouraged and sad at times. That's part of our human nature. We tend to roll with the tide and suffer ups and downs. But, we bounce back because we have hope that things will get better and, with Christ's help, they do.

Bill White was one of those who passed into eternity with His Lord on July 20th. What an incredible man he was to anyone who knew him. He is one of whom it can be said, "He was true to himself." He never pretended to be something he wasn't. He lived life to the fullest. His wife, his children and his grandchildren as well as his siblings, nieces, nephews and many friends adored him. During his "Graduation Celebration" we laughed a great deal, remembering some of the events of his life that touched other lives. He will be greatly missed.

The other friend was one of the sweetest saints I've ever known, Mary Williams. I never heard her say an unkind word about anything or anyone. But, Mary suffered for years with arthritic pain and knowing she will no longer have to tolerate that is a blessing. Now she has gained her reward. Her sweet spirit will also be missed by all who knew her.

Just as we overuse the word 'love' to describe all sorts of feelings, we use 'hope' lackadaisically, too. I hope that tomorrow won't be so hot. I hope I get a raise this year. I hope I lose weight this year. I hope my kids come see me. I hope this and I hope that. The fact is that without hope, we do become depressed. Hoping for something better keeps us going... something to look forward to.

Have you ever noticed how depressed you get listening to someone who complains continually? That person can find something negative to say about just about everything. On the other hand, think of a friend who is always upbeat, accepting circumstances as if they are nothing. Which friend would you rather spend time with?

Having hope is very much like that. We can accept the fact something better will happen or we can sink into depression, believing there is no hope for a better tomorrow.

The Bible speaks often of hope and its value in our lives. Here are just a few verses expressing the hope we have.

Wherefore gird up the loins of your mind, be sober, and hope to the end for the grace that is to be brought unto you at the revelation of Jesus Christ. (I Peter 1:13)

Be of good courage, and he shall strengthen your heart, all ye that hope in the Lord. (Psalm 31:24)

For thou art my hope, O Lord God: thou are my trust from my youth. (Psalm 71:5)

I will hope continually... (Psalm 71:14a)

It is good that a man should both hope and quietly wait for the salvation of the Lord. (Lamentations 3:26)

The Promise of Hope

Without hope, what is there? Each day it becomes harder to have hope in the future. Every day there is some story about a tragedy or a catastrophe such as wildfires in Southern California. The news was especially heartbreaking when we learned that arson was involved in at least two of the fires. What causes a person's psyche to even think in such a way?

The news about the prevalence of a 'candy' drug for young children was unbelievable. In Dallas, Texas a scheme was uncovered to trick youngsters into trying the new 'candy' and discovered that for some it only took one trial to cause a death. Those behind the idea were garnering thousands of dollars because their product was so cheap.

A school board in Maine voted to give birth control pills to middle school aged children without the parents' knowledge. The original story stated the vote was 5-2 but that was wrong. It was 7-2. It also stated condoms were first offered in 2002. Actually, it was 2000. With a state law that says it is illegal to have sex for anyone under 14, what is wrong with this school board? Some parents were outraged but, to my amazement, some were not. Now we know that this is not the first school in the country to offer this "protection" to under-aged children.

When I was in high school, we were shown

films about syphilis and gonorrhea to remind us of the dangers of immoral sexual activity. That worked for most of the students. And, yes, abstinence was encouraged. Not so today. Such teaching isn't allowed. "It's not realistic," opponents say.

A TV documentary entitled, *Facing Reality: Choices,* followed three young women who were pregnant. Two of the women were never married but had no trouble conceiving. One decided to abort her baby because her boyfriend was not willing to help her. This was her second abortion in a year. Another woman who was addicted to drugs was carrying her seventh child. She finally decided to get clean and keep this baby as she had lost custody of the others. She miscarried. The third woman was married and desperately wanted children. She had one son and was pregnant with a little girl. When told her baby would probably die soon after birth because of a defect, she and her husband decided to go ahead with the pregnancy to at least "give the baby a chance." The baby died just before birth.

We can't help but ask, "Why? Why do bad things happen to good people?"

Years ago, politicians were regarded with utmost respect. After all, they are our leaders. We want, and expect, them to operate with honesty. But, that was years ago. It appears today that no new scandal even fazes us. We are no longer shocked to read about another unfortunate figure caught red-handed. Where is the shame?

Lying used to be frowned upon. Nowadays, the person who is the best liar is the one who is believed and held up as an example for all to emulate. If someone tries to get the truth out, guess who is persecuted?

Is it possible to have hope in anything or anybody anymore?

Yes, I believe it is. Years ago after Xenia, Ohio was wiped out by a tornado, it was rebuilt and is better than ever. Even Hiroshima which was bombed to oblivion is now thriving with unbelievable beauty. Sometimes good does come out of bad. If it doesn't, we need to turn to the greatest book on earth, the Bible, to restore our hope. In it we learn that this world is not our final home, that we are pilgrims passing through to a better place.

Poor Job bemoaned, **My days are spent without hope** (Job 7:6) but God restored everything to him twofold except for the number of children. The psalmist stated, **My hope is in thee.** (Psalm 39:7) The preacher in Ecclesiastes declared, **For to him that is joined to all the living there is hope.** (Ecclesiastes 9:4) Jeremiah, referred to as the "weeping prophet," assured us that, **Blessed is the man that trusteth in the Lord, and whose hope the Lord is.** (Jeremiah 17:7) Paul told the Romans, **We are saved by hope.** (Romans 8:24)

A verse quoted often at funerals comes from

I Corinthians wherein Paul wrote, *If in this life only we have hope in Christ, we are of all men most miserable.* (I Corinthians 15:19) In other words, our hope is not in this life. There are better things waiting for us who have hope in Christ.

The writer of Hebrews refers to hope as *an anchor to our soul.* (Hebrews 6:19) And, finally, Peter told us what our response should be when asked about our hope. *Be ready always to give an answer to every man that asketh you a reason of the hope that is in you with meekness and fear.* (I Peter 3:15)

As stated earlier, it is easy to become disheartened when we read and see the events taking place daily. Christ came to take away our sins and to restore us to God. Take heart, my friend, because the dessert (the best) is yet to come.

True Love

What is true love? Is there such a thing? Many people believe they can answer, 'Yes' because they have experienced it. Others would scoff at the idea of love at all. What a shame!

February is the month known for 'love' and showers of such expression are doled out in abundance. The practice started back in the third century when St. Valentine, a priest, decided to disobey a Roman decree by Claudius and marry couples who were in love. For this he was put to death on February 14, 269 A.D. Two hundred and thirty years later, Pope Gelasius set aside February 14 to honour Valentine and the date became known as the time for lovers to send messages to one another.

It wasn't until the 1800s in the United States when the commercializing of card giving on Valentine's Day became a tradition. The post office of Loveland, Colorado is inundated every year with an increased business in February.

From the Internet I learned that, "In the Middle Ages, young men and women drew names from a bowl to see who their valentines would be. They would wear these names on their sleeves for one week. To wear your heart on your sleeve now means that it is easy for other people to know how you are feeling."

Another superstition was, "Some people used to believe that if a woman saw a robin flying overhead on Valentine's Day, it meant she would marry a sailor. If she saw a sparrow, she would marry a poor man and be very happy. If she saw a goldfinch, she would marry a millionaire."

As a child, more than once I did the following: "Think of five or six names of boys or girls you might marry. As you twist the stem of an apple, recite the names until the stem comes off. You will marry the person whose name you were saying when the stem fell off." You know something? That almost came true, in a sense. My husband's first name began with the letter I always repeated. Of course, I was thinking of the last name of a certain boy back then.

Getting back to what is true love, the Bible gives us the only real answer when we read, **For God so loved the world he gave his only begotten son that whosoever believeth on him should not perish but have everlasting life.** (John 3:16) That is "Agape" or "True Love!" Christ's commandment to us is **Love one another as I have loved you.** (John 15:12)

When Generosity Really Counts

I learned about tithing as a child. During the Depression, even a dollar bill was a lot of money. However, my father and mother were believers and practiced tithing 10% of every dollar. Over the years, that 10% grew as Daddy's income increased.

I heard a story once about a man who complained to his minister that since he was making more money, he was expected to give more to the church. The minister asked him, "Would you rather go back to the days when you weren't making as much money as you are now?"

In Luke 6:38 we read, **Give, and it shall be given unto you; good measure, pressed down, and shaken together, and running over, shall men give into your bosom. For with the same measure that ye mete withal it shall be measured to you again.** Wow! What a promise!

Wait just a minute! "You mean to tell me I should give to someone else when I have bills to pay?" The answer, of course, is "No, you have a duty to pay your bills first." The problem arises when we rack up unnecessary bills due to our insatiable "wants." Since the appearance of the credit card, it's been too easy to satisfy our wants instead of paying for our needs first.

Many years ago our family, along with my parents, took a trip to Ohio for Thanksgiving.

After visiting with family, we thought it would be great to go on to Washington, D.C. since we knew we would soon be moving back to the west coast. Because of bad weather we were delayed and we barely made it home, literally with prayer and a little change in our pockets. If credit cards had been available, we would not have worried, but this was before credit cards or ATMs and cashing a personal check in another state was out of the question over a holiday weekend. Our "wants" almost left us stranded.

I remember a dear lady who gave over $90,000 to pay off a debt after a church split had occurred and two-thirds of the congregation left without paying their promised pledges. Without her generous gift, the church might have been forced to close its doors. Because of her gift, God is blessing that church. She was not your "normal" philanthropist who gave out of an abundance of finances. She'd been frugal her whole life and now was an elderly widow with no family to support her. But she believed God wanted her to help the church and, if she did, he would continue to bless her. He did!

He will bless you, too, because it truly is **more blessed to give than to receive**. (Acts 20:35)

Why Not Sin?

What is the one thing in the whole world that everybody has done, is doing and will do? For anyone who has ever attended Sunday School, that's easy...SIN! Isaiah was the first to tell us that **all have sinned** and that no one is perfect. Paul repeats the sad news when he wrote to the Romans. **For all have sinned and come short of the glory of God**. (Romans 3:23) What that means is, we're all in the same boat, whether we are rich or poor, young or old, Gentile or Jew, black or white. We ALL have sinned. In I John 1:8 we read, **If we say that we have no sin, we deceive ourselves, and the truth is not in us**.

The good news is there is a way to redeem ourselves. **If we confess our sins, he is faithful and just to forgive us our sins, and to cleanse us from all unrighteousness**. (I John 1:9) Whew! What a relief! But, the next problem arises because it's so hard to admit our sin even to ourselves. Unless we do, we're lost.

So, why is it then that when we admit our sin and ask for forgiveness, bad things still happen? The fact remains that *we* can be forgiven but *sin always has consequences*! That's one of the worst parts about sin. Although we can be washed *"white as snow"* as if we never sinned, the consequences of our sin are not. The Bible warns us in Galatians 6:7 with this admonition:

Be not deceived; God is not mocked: for whatsoever a man soweth, that shall he also reap.

I watched an interview with Charles (Chuck) Colson, the founder of Prison Ministries. I remember when he was one of President Nixon's henchmen, willing to do "whatever" for the president…and he did. But he saw the error of his ways, repented and gave his life to Christ. While serving time in prison, he saw a great need and thus we now have Prison Ministries. There are *always* blessings that follow obedience no matter what crime or sin has been committed. Colson has since written numerous books and gives his whole life over to making a change for the better. What an example he is for everyone who calls himself/herself a Christian!

Some have said that God isn't fair because the Bible tells us that anyone can be forgiven, even the worst kind of criminal. That's true but we read in Revelation 22:7 that ***…whosever will, let him take the water of life freely.*** Look at David's life; or Paul's. Both committed terrible crimes and yet after repenting, God embraced them. The decision is ours to make.

After witnessing to a neighbor, she told me that, "When I get old, I'll think about it." The problem with that kind of thinking is that sometimes people don't have a chance to "get old." God can take us at any time and at any age. It's dangerous to wait until you're old and then say to yourself, "I guess I better make things right with the Lord before I die." Accidents happen. Sudden death happens. None of us knows when our time here on earth is over. It's best to be prepared, as the Boy Scouts motto says. Why? Because, **It is a fearful thing to fall into the hands of the living God.** (Hebrews 10:31)

A story is told about a baseball player, turned preacher, by the name of Billy Sunday over a century ago. He was asked by a young man at the end of one of his fire and brimstone sermons, "What if you're wrong? What if there is no hereafter?"

The answer was, "If there isn't, I've lived a good life and will have no regrets. But, let me ask you, 'What if I'm right? Where will you be?'"

To reiterate, **For the wages of sin is death; but the gift of God is eternal life through Jesus Christ our Lord.** (Romans 6:23)

Why Repent?

Years ago I worked for a government agency that offered social welfare to needy families. Most of the time the need was for financial help but oftentimes the need was for guidance. Some people just couldn't live peacefully with other humans. When worry and frustration take over, a person becomes disgruntled to the point of taking their anger out on whoever is nearby. Then, after the storm, they say...for the umpteen time, "I'm sorry. It won't happen again." Too often the offended party quickly forgives and all is calm until the next blowup. Tragedies happen when someone's anger takes over once too often.

Today many families are going through tremendous trials because of the economy. Lack of jobs means a lack of finances and a lack of finances leads to bad behavior. And so the cycle goes.

For those of us who lived during the Great Depression when we literally existed on a hand to mouth basis, we can understand the turmoil many people have now. However, back then we didn't realize how bad off we were. In spite of the circumstances, we pulled together, helping whoever and wherever we could.

When I ask myself why that was so, I come up with one major reason: *We trusted in God to see us through.* Our parents applied Christ's message to: **Seek ye first the kingdom of God** *and His righteousness and all these things will be added unto you.* (Matthew 6:33) In order to do that, one has to be willing to acknowledge there is a God, confess a belief in Him, accept the gift of His son, Jesus Christ, and repent of his sins. When the Apostle Peter who was asked what they (the people) should do to be saved, he replied, *Repent and be baptized, every one of you, in the name of Jesus Christ for the forgiveness of your sins, and you will receive the gift of the Holy Spirit.* (Acts 2:38)

In today's world, too many people are unwilling to humble themselves to seek God's help. They cannot forgive and therefore are not ready to repent of their ways. We humans, created by God, need to look at Christ's sacrifice and ask ourselves, "If he was willing to be tortured, humiliated and die for us (asking God to forgive his persecutors even while he languished in pain), shouldn't we be willing to at least consider his gift of eternal life?" Such a repentant heart is rewarded with joy and peace.

Part Two

Our Part

Acceptance...Just As I Am

Popeye said, "I am what I am and that's all that I am." We loved him for his bravery and strength, the latter because he ate his spinach. I've often heard people state, "I am what I am and you can take it or leave it." They have no intention of improving any flaws they have.

On the other hand, there are some who never think they can be "good enough" to be accepted by Christ. They have done too many 'bad things' to even ask for forgiveness. Both thoughts are wrong.

The Bible tells us that *...**we should be holy and blameless before Him.*** (Ephesians 1:4b) Since all humans are sinful, how can we expect to be holy? Drop down to verse 7 and we have our answer. **In Him we have redemption through His blood, the forgiveness of our trespasses, according to the riches of His grace.** God *always* provides a way for us to escape our sinful ways.

Billy Graham never ended his vast services without offering an altar call while the choir sang, *Just As I Am*. Charlotte Elliott was a young lady who rejected Christianity and was insulted when asked if she were a Christian. She responded angrily but as she reflected upon the question and her reaction, she went back to the questioner to ask how she could become a Christian. The elderly man said, "Come just as you are." She did and in 1835 wrote the hymn known all over the world.

The last verse says it all. *Just as I am, Thou wilt receive, Wilt welcome, pardon, cleanse, relieve, Because Thy promise I believe, O Lamb of God, I come! I come!* (Source: Signs of the Times, Copyright © July 26, 1942, Pacific Press.)

Trouble comes when we are unwilling to accept His forgiveness. Our pride, stubbornness, rebellion and selfishness keep us from embracing God's wonderful gift of salvation. The beauty is we don't have to wait until we clean up our act. After all, we'll never be perfect as long as we breathe. It takes some of us longer to relinquish our negative habits and attitudes but once we do we wonder what kept us from seeing the Light of the World, Jesus. There is nothing to compare with the **peace that passeth all understanding** (Philippians 4:7) and that only comes from knowing Christ as our Lord and Savior.

An Army slogan states *Be all that you can be.* That's what we should strive for as Christians…to be the best that we can be. That means changing some of our ways. Once we start, the changes continue throughout our lifetime.

Ah, Patience

Ah, Patience! Wherefore art thou? Many of us could ask that question several times during a day. We seem to have inherited a need to hurry. We don't learn from the oft repeated, "Haste makes waste."

Isn't that what causes "road rage?" You're running late and trying to take it easy and flow with the traffic but someone ahead of you is in the fast lane going five miles under the allowed speed limit. There's no way to pass because the slow lane is already occupied. Do you sit back patiently, realizing there's no way you can change things or do you get upset and irritated?

Plant a seed and take note of how often you check to see the first sprout.

Go to a doctor's office for an appointment but be sure to take along some reading material so your blood pressure won't go overboard once you finally enter the examining room.

After surgery a patient seldom wants to simply lie around, especially if that person is normally quite active and energetic. "Take your time. Don't overdo," advises the doctor. That's hard to do once one starts feeling well.

Try watching a youngster barely able to hold a spoon feed himself. You want to help him get the food into his mouth, but no. This child is independent and wants to do it himself! Frustrating? Yes, for some of us. For others, endowed with loving patience, they enjoy watching the growing process of seeing someone so small develop new abilities. They don't mind the mess that usually occurs.

Did you notice I used the term "loving patience?" That's because it takes love to be patient. In fact, someone years ago wrote, "Impatience is a lack of love." I, in my hurry up way, had never thought of that. It made me stop and think and realize it is true. If we show consideration and patience toward someone trying to learn something new, we are exercising a type of love and caring.

The easiest way to learn anything is to do it yourself. When I first sat down to a computer, it scared me to death. I was afraid to touch a key because I knew so little about how it worked. Thankfully, I had someone to lean on who was so patient, I soon began to venture further. The one thing she said over and over was, "Take your time. Don't hurry. Think about what you're doing." My biggest problem was that, once I learned just a little, I began to hurry, clicking keys too soon. Then her comment was, "S l-o-w down. Read what it says."

When I had the opportunity to teach seniors how to use a computer, a comment I often heard after a session was, "Thanks for being so patient with me." I told them I understood because I was once in their shoes, too.

"But," you ask, "What does all that have to do

with spirituality?" My answer is, "A great deal!" Have you ever stopped to realize that time is the one commodity given to everyone equally and we are not to waste it! **Redeeming the time because the days are evil.** (Ephesians 5:16) There is a time for everything. **To every thing there is a season, and time to every purpose under the heaven.** (Ecclesiastes 3:1). Some things take more time than others.

The farmer plants his crop and in due time, he reaps a harvest.

Someone greets you with a broad smile and in a split second you're happier.

The prophets patiently warned the Israelites many times over about the sins they committed against the Lord God. Isaiah foretold the coming Messiah 700 years before He appeared.

We read about "the patience of Job" because the devil was allowed to test him beyond most people's endurance. By remaining steadfast to his Lord, he was blessed more in the end than he was before his loss and suffering.

Teachers who take the time to work with their students to make sure they fully understand a problem are rewarded when they see their pupils develop.

Of course, there are some people who are so unlovable, it's difficult to be patient and loving toward them. But, they are the very ones who especially need it. That's when I have to remember, **Whoever loves God must also love**

his brother. (I John 4:21) What a hard pill to swallow. That is, until I realize that I've made it hard for God to love me at times. Yet, He has and will continue to show patience and love toward me as long as I repent when I falter.

Well, Rome wasn't built in a day so perhaps there's still hope for me.

A Purity

A few years ago when I volunteered as a reader for the SMART program, one of my students was an adorable Mexican boy in first grade. Although I wanted to give him a "grandma" hug (because he was so cute) we were told not to touch the children in any way.

Each child was allowed to choose a couple of books to read and one day he said, "How about a Spanish book?" I replied, "I don't know. It's been a long time since I've read any Spanish." But he insisted, "Well, you can try." So, he chose a book, we found our reading spot and I proceeded to read the first line. That's as far as I got because he took the book from me and said, "You're right. You can't read Spanish." I have laughed about that ever since. The pure honesty of a child is so endearing.

It's been said that a child under eight and an adult over 80 can say just about anything and you know they are speaking the truth. The child speaks from innocence; the adult from experience. Kind adults will taper their comments with some diplomacy but not the child.

The same can be said about children being loving. They have an inborn trust which can be dangerous. No wonder Christ admonished his disciples when he said, **Suffer little children and forbid them not to come unto me: for of**

such is the kingdom of heaven. (Matthew 19:14) He wants everyone to come to him with the innocence of a child-like nature.

A new perspective about purity occurred to me as I read a devotional about Elisha. He was surrounded by enemies which were seen by those with him. But, Elisha also saw the Lord's army. He had "spiritual vision." Myopia is an eye problem wherein we do not see clearly. In the devotional the writer related our 'spiritual myopia' as a deficiency in many Christian's lives. We concentrate on worldly matters and get bogged down with worry and frustration. If we would concentrate on God's promises, we could see clearly and believe that ***all things work together for good to those who love God and are called according to his purpose.*** (Romans 8:28)

Remember the silversmith who was asked how he could tell when his product was just right? He answered, "When I can see myself in it I know it's pure." When others can see God in us, we are being purified by Christ. We won't reach that final stage of purification until we see Him face to face in heaven but we must continue to strive for perfection.

Be Ye Kind, One to Another

When upsetting events happen in our lives because of what someone has done to us, it's mighty hard to "turn the other cheek" or to obey what Paul wrote in Ephesians 4:32: **Be ye kind one to another, tenderhearted, forgiving one another, even as God for Christ's sake hath forgiven you.** Most human beings are not naturally adept at forgiving. There have been many times when I've wanted to fight back. Even if we don't strike back at unjust assaults, it's nigh on impossible to forgive sometimes. Unfortunately, there are people who are naturally unkind and we need to accept that's their problem, not ours.

If I consider how the only Perfect One who ever lived was horribly tortured through no fault of his, it causes me to reflect on my problem and compare it to what Christ endured. Every time I do I come up short because *there is no comparison*. No matter how badly we're treated, we will *never* suffer as Christ did. We should focus on those among us who are kind and thoughtful, some going out of their way to do for others, oftentimes what they cannot do for themselves.

There's a song that says, "Little things mean a lot." In the park where I live, more than once when I've taken my garbage to the dumpster, one of the men of the before-feminism-took-over-generation will come up and say, "Here, let me take that for you." Yes, even the "little things mean a lot."

In a book of quotations one on "kindness" stated, *Kindness consists of loving people more than they deserve* by Joseph Joubert. It reminded me of a story I read years ago about a lady in a mental hospital who was most difficult to handle. She was not just unattractive, she was ugly. Her disposition matched her looks and no one wanted to tend to her. One day an attendant decided she would make the effort to love the patient. She began befriending her in little ways at first and gradually the patient began to respond. The story had a happy ending because the loving care drew the patient out of her morbid and hateful attitude.

Dr. Tim LaHaye spoke at a Christian Women's luncheon I attended once. A young wife asked him, "What can I do to get my husband to be nicer to me and to help me?" Dr. LaHaye answered, "Treat him like a king and eventually he will respond to you as you show love to him." Whether that story had a successful ending or not it seemed like good advice and many of us went home to apply the technique ourselves.

An acquaintance related how she spent two nights a week teaching inmates for two hours at the county jail in her area. When asked if they really learned or were simply attending to get credit, she said, "Yes. Some did respond to the caring effort. One even earned his GED while there."

Everyone seems to be concerned these days about what his/her legacy will be after death. Another quotation in my devotional book states, *It is a man's kindly acts that are remembered of him in the years after his life.* Ptah-hotep said that. It started me thinking about people I have known over the years and what people say about them, especially at their memorial service. I have yet to hear anything unkind about the departed at such a time. Just the opposite because the comments are all about the good memories of that person. I jokingly told my pastor that anyone could say anything at my memorial service, but stipulated, *"as long as it is good!"*

Our Lord admonished us to be kind to one another and the old saying is so true: *You can catch more flies with honey than with vinegar!* The world would be so much better if more people practiced that philosophy.

Breastplate of Righteousness

Being "righteous" must have been important to God because that word, or words derived from it, is mentioned throughout the scriptures. To think of "righteousness" reminds me of the opposite, "sin" and "judgment."

When Saul was trying to kill David and David had an opportunity to kill him but didn't, Saul cried out, **Thou art more righteous than I.** Speaking of David, he was quite a man. We first learn of him as a young shepherd who played beautiful, soothing music for the king. He went on to be a mighty warrior before dying as an old man. In the intervening years he demonstrated how good...and yes, righteous....a person can be as well as how evil man can be. Yet, the Bible tells us that God said David was **a man after my heart.** How could that be? Besides all the good David did, he was also an adulterer and a murderer. David composed a beautiful psalm that gives us the answer. In Psalm 51:4 we read, **Against you, you only, have I sinned and done what is evil in your sight.** All the bad things we do...sinful things...are against God because He's the Only Perfect One. There is no righteousness apart from God.

Look at Solomon, the wisest man who ever lived apart from Christ Himself so we're told. Now, I ask you, would a truly wise man have 300 wives and 700 concubines? Yet, God blessed him with great wisdom in the beginning of his realm because *in humility* Solomon asked God for wisdom, not *things.* Because of that, God blessed him with great riches as well. Too bad Solomon didn't remain focused on God.

Who hasn't known someone who personifies self-righteous? Someone who believes he never makes a mistake? Someone who readily judges others? About such a person Christ admonished, **How can you say to your brother, 'Let me take the speck out of your eye,' when all the time there is a plank in your own eye? You hypocrite, first take the plank out of your own eye, and then you will see clearly to remove the speck from your brother's eye.** (Matthew 7:4,5)

Does that mean we humans can never be "righteous?" Of course not. We are instructed to be righteous several times in scripture. But, our righteousness *must come from God* because He is the Only One Who is righteous.

And then, there is humility. Have you ever read a book entitled, *Humility and How I Achieved It?* Well, duh! How "humble" would such an author be? The fact is we must rely on God to endow us with the spirit of righteousness and truth as well as humility.

When Paul wrote to the Colossians he gave them instructions we all can follow today. **And whatsoever ye do, do it heartily, as to the Lord, and not unto men; Knowing that of the Lord ye shall receive the reward of the inher- -itance; for ye serve the Lord Christ.**

(Colossians 3:23, 24) We can do that by putting on the **breastplate of righteousness** about which Paul wrote. (Ephesians 6:14).

Contentment IS Possible

Every newscast and headline blares out words to the effect that "The sky is falling," reminding us of Chicken Little in the children's story. Gloom and doom spring forth in nearly all aspects of life. Terrorists have gripped people with fear. Where might they strike next? In what way? Children are killing children as if it were a game. Can't they tell real life from make believe? Or, are they hurting so much they don't care? Much of entertainment is no longer entertainment. The more obscene and violent, so much the better appears to be the desired theme. In the rare instances when a good, funny movie is released, people hungrily swarm to see it. Contented? Who can possibly be content in this day and age?

History tells us that power doesn't bring contentment. Every sovereign that existed wanted more. The more they acquired, the more they sought. They were never satisfied. Today we see people dying of hunger in lands where the hierarchies live lavishly, ignoring those in need. Greed reigns supreme with eyes closed. Still, they aren't content.

Fame, too, has been found to be a poor substitute for contentment. How sad to see the so-called "beautiful" people who either turn their lives upside down, seeking that evasive "something" that could give them happiness. Or, worse yet, those who end up taking their lives because they can no longer stand the pain of unhappiness.

Money? "If only I had more money," is often uttered, especially toward the end of the month. But, what does the Bible tell us about that? How sad the rich man was who walked away from Christ after Christ told him to go sell all he had and give to the poor. Years ago we toured the Hearst Castle in California and the guide told us about the expensive items Mr. Hearst had collected from all over the world. The one thought that ran through my mind was the Bible verse from Matthew 16:26 where Christ asked, ***For what is a man profited, if he shall gain the whole world, and lose his own soul?*** Those who have lost savings during this recent downturn need to keep that in mind. No amount of money can save anyone. Nor can it bring happiness. Striving for more has not been the answer.

Too many have learned the "grass is" *not* "greener on the other side." A new mate does not bring about the desired joy the person was seeking. Consequently, half of the marriages today end in divorce and many children suffer through no fault of their own.

Even we Christians are guilty of abusing our bodies with drugs and, yes, gluttony. Ever been to a church potluck? Then we wonder why we're sickly. The Apostle Paul told the Corinthians that. **...you are not your own. For you are bought with a price: therefore glorify God in your body, and in your spirit, which are God's.** (I Corinthians 6:19b-20)

Indeed, it is difficult to even imagine oneself being content if one is aware of all the grief and destruction surrounding us. St. Francis of Assisi gave a good answer to the question, "How can I be content?" when he wrote:

God, grant me the serenity to accept the things I cannot change,
Courage to change the things I can,
Wisdom to know the difference.

If only we could make that philosophy a part of our own, how much happier we would be!

While in prison, the Apostle Paul declared, **Not that I speak in respect of want: for I have learned, in whatsoever state I am, therewith to be content.** (Philippians 4:11) His prison wasn't exactly a Hotel Hilton either. Yet, he didn't spend his time bemoaning his condition nor circumstances. He preached to his guards, converting them into becoming believers in Christ.

Over 50 years ago, the songwriter, Johnny Lange wrote a song entitled, *I Found The Answer.* In it he tells how he struggled through the darkness until he couldn't go on. Then he *found the answer* because he *learned to pray*! Many of us have sung the song about Jesus being *only a prayer away.* That is so true. When all else fails, He's right there ready to pick up the pieces of our lives and put us back together again. That's when contentment sets in...when we put Christ in charge of our life. We will never be perfect as long as we breathe the air of this earth, but He promises to help us get back on our feet and able to go on when we stumble along life's highway.

After watching the video, *The Medical Aspects of the Crucifixion,* wherein Dr. Jameso Fuzzell, a medical doctor, explained precisely how Christ must have suffered when He was crucified, I realized Christ didn't just die. He truly agonized in a torturous manner we can't even fathom. The good doctor believes that, in the end, because of the physical aspects Christ's body endured, He literally died of a broken heart because His heart must have exploded.

He had good reason to die of a broken heart. Mankind has always been selfish, greedy and inhumane. The fact Christ loves us so much He was *willing* to die in that way so we might have eternal life in heaven is incomprehensible to this human mind. However, as the old hymn says, *"My hope is built on nothing less than Jesus' love and righteousness"* for which I am most grateful and, consequently, have learned to be content.

Do the Right Thing

Many years ago, but still during my lifetime, it was not uncommon for men to confirm a deal with a handshake. Imagine! One man would tell another what he would do and the other would agree on the price. At that point, they shook hands, and the contract was sealed. Neither man would have dreamed of breaking the contract.

As a child, we oftentimes crossed our heart and hoped to die if we broke our word. We meant it, too. Some brave kids would prick their finger to make a "blood commitment" but not me! I have never liked needles or blood!

What has happened in our world today? Schoolteachers have lost their jobs because they attempted to instill a 'no-cheating' system in their classrooms. Instead of parents agreeing to the discipline, they complained.

In Houston, Texas a Key Middle School teacher attempted to report cheating after too many students scored high scores on TAKS (Texas Assessment of Knowledge and Skills) test. Nothing was done about it, however, because the top lawyer refused to grant the teacher immunity from punishment! That's right! The teacher would have been punished if she pursued the allegation. There's something wrong with that picture.

A second year cadet at the Air Force Academy

resigned when he was found cheating along with six other cadets. He was one of their star athletes. Now, a black mark is on his record. Four of the other cadets were cleared because there was insufficient evidence to prove the case.

In Korea, test scores from 312 students were declared invalid by BAI (Board of Adult and Inspection) due to cheating so obviously this 'disease' is not just prevalent here in America.

The Internet provides a wealth of information and some of it is true. I was appalled when I read *Cheating 101 for Private Schools.*

On that same website I found links such as, *Infidelity Investigator, Cheating, How to Survive Cheating, Catch a Cheating Lover.*

Of course, there are numerous ways of cheating and one of the busiest times of the year for it is coming up when people file their tax returns.

The opposite trait from cheating is integrity so I thought it would be helpful to read how some of the great people of the Bible felt about that. When Job was being tempted by the devil and his friends tried to tell him he must have done something wrong, time and again he kept his integrity. Even when his wife asked him, **Dost thou still retain thine integrity? Curse God, and die**, he remained steadfast. After Bildad tried to convince him that man cannot be justified before God, Job replied, **God forbid that I should justify you: till I die I will not** *remove my integrity from me.*

In Psalm 8 David pleads with the Lord to...*judge me according to mine integrity that is in me.* Later in Psalm 25 he prays, **Let integrity and uprightness preserve me; for I wait on thee**.

The Preacher in Proverbs admonishes, **Better is the poor that walketh in his integrity than he that is perverse in his lips and is a fool.** (Proverbs 28:6)

Today the courts are overflowing with frivolous lawsuits because people are out to get something for nothing. After my husband retired from a service-type business, he often said, "I'm sure glad I'm no longer in business. People are just waiting to sue for no reason whatever."

At the time my father started his construction business, there were few papers that needed to be signed. Now, we are warned to have a real estate lawyer check over all papers proffered when buying a home.

It's as if we are like the three monkeys who, with their eyes, ears and mouth covered, "see no evil", "hear no evil" and "speak no evil". The saying that you "Can't believe anything you hear and only half of what you read" doesn't apply anymore. We can't believe almost everything we hear or read. I doubt if we will ever return to "the good old days" when a man's word meant something, but it would be nice if we could believe *something* we're told. There's still hope.

Faith Is....

Faith is turning a switch on and expecting to flood the room with light. Faith is turning the key in the ignition and expecting your car to start. Faith is stopping at a stop sign and expecting others to do likewise. Faith is running the tap and expecting clear, clean water to come out. Faith is expecting people to be honest. Faith is writing a check and expecting the electronic funds to be there in your account to cover it.

Yes, faith in our common, every day language is a lot of things. But, what is faith according to the Bible? **Faith is the substance of things hoped for and the evidence of things not seen** we read in Hebrews 11:1. Think about it...**the substance of things hoped for.** In this day and age, there's probably no soul who is not hoping for better things. The constant drone of war with its casualties, the sight of war torn countries, the news of corruption is sickening.

How should a Christian face the every day doom and gloom? With a happy heart, that's how! Why? Because we *know* there are better things in store for us. I marvel whenever I read about countries that are saturated with devastation due to war and yet see that people are turning to the Lord in droves. He is their only hope! They have no "evidence" that things will be better, but they have "hope" in the promises given.

The following is copied from a mission bulletin. *In Eritrea, an African country on the Red Sea, a crackdown on young Christians is going on! Many have been arrested and subjected to "Punishment for their crimes." Some have been locked in metal shipping containers in heat and dark. All have been ordered to sign a denial of their faith. Those refusing have had food withheld. 230 Christians are known to be prisoners for the FAITH!*

One of my favorite hymns begins with the words *My hope is built on nothing less than Jesus' love and righteousness.* The title of that hymn is *The Solid Rock.* Christians are blessed, no matter what befalls them because we have THE SOLID ROCK! There is nothing nor no one that can take that away from us. We have a secure foundation.

The evidence of saving faith is not how much you believe but how well you behave, is a quote from *The Daily Walk* of September 26, 2003. Going through a particularly hard struggle at the time I read that, I had to ask myself, How am I showing I have a solid, secure foundation of faith in Christ? Am I like the people who were praying for Peter's release from prison but were stunned when he actually showed up? Or, am I showing the kind of faith the woman had who was healed from a 12-year bleeding problem by merely touching Jesus' garment? Too often I would be among those of whom Christ said, **Oh ye of little faith**.

Of course, when I read how the disciples, who traveled with Jesus in person, still struggled to believe, it eases my mind momentarily...but it doesn't excuse me any more than it did them. Every trial that comes our way should cause us to exercise our faith that eventually all will work out in *God's way* and in *His time.* We are not promised our wants, only our needs. Knowing, and believing that, brings comfort.

In a daily devotional from Bill Keller, a pastor in Florida, he wrote the following: "We often can't understand why tragedies befall good people, often totally innocent people. Again, it is times like these that our faith must become real, we must trust that God is still on the throne. And while we don't always understand why, we know ultimately His will, His plan and purpose will play out. While we all have doubts at different times in our life, the answer to those doubts is our faith in God."

I heard an African-born missionary who said, "It takes love to solve the problems of Aids," so prevalent in his native country. "But," he went on, "it all starts from the heart. Without the heart, there can be no love. Without the heart, there can be no faith."

Yes, indeed, real faith is a <u>necessity</u> for a Christian for we read in Hebrews 11:6, **But without faith it is impossible to please him: for he that cometh to God must believe that he is, and that he is a rewarder of them that diligently seek him.**

Forgiving

"*The heaviest load any man carries on his back is a pack of grudges*" is a quote from the June 3, 2002 Daily Walk devotional booklet. People have made themselves sick because of a grudge they hold against someone. Oftentimes, the feeling of ill will is deserved. People have, indeed, been mistreated in some way. But, who gets hurt? The one who holds the grudge, not the person who causes it. Sometimes, in fact, the guilty party is unaware he has done or said anything wrong.

Far too often this happens in families. A misunderstanding arises and through pride no one is willing to take the step of healing. "I'm sorry" seems to be two of the hardest words to speak. On Father's Day, 2002, Dr. James Kennedy of the Coral Ridge Ministry in Florida talked about the importance of having a right relationship in the home. He ended his sermon by requesting that the wives and husbands find something good about their spouse to tell him/her every day for the next week. He said there had been something to first attract them to one another and to think of what that might be. Then, start building again the good feelings they had in the beginning.

There's a story going around about 'How to have a happy marriage.' Seems the wife told her husband when they returned from their honeymoon that she was going to put a box on their closet shelf that was hers only. "You are never to look in it," she told him. He never did.

Then, when they were elderly, she became ill and the doctor told him she wasn't going to live much longer. He went to his wife and said, "Honey, don't you think I should look in that box on the shelf?" She agreed and he brought it to her. Inside were two doilies and $25,000. He was amazed and asked her to explain the contents.

"When we were first married, my aunt told me that, if I wanted a happy marriage, I should make a doily every time I got angry with you. So, I did." His eyes welled up with tears just thinking about the fact she had only gotten angry twice in all the years they had been married. Then he asked her about the $25,000. "Oh," she said, "that's the money I got for selling doilies."

Within a work environment there are those who will do anything to get ahead. They will lie or cheat. Their goal is to get ahead and nothing stops them. We need to realize we do not live in a perfect world. As we grow older this fact becomes more evident and accepting. We learn that everything is not equal, nor is everyone.

"Love one another as I have loved you," admonished Christ in John 15:12. Easy to say, but very hard to do. Some people just are not lovable. For example the despicable terrorists who have already harmed America (and other countries) in unspeakable ways and some who continue planning further treacherous acts. "You mean, we are to love THEM? No way!"

But, what does the Bible teach? ***Love your enemies, bless them that curse you, do good to them that hate you, and pray*** (the key word) ***for them which despitefully use you, and persecute you*** we read in Matthew 5:44. ***With men this is impossible, but with God all things are possible*** according to Matthew 19:26. Again, the words of Christ when He said in Mark 11:26, ***But if you do not forgive, neither will your father who is in heaven forgive you your trespasses.***

In other words, as a Christian, I am commanded to forgive others so that I might be forgiven of my sins. My pastor, Dr. Aaron Veach, said we should always remember the following: *I am a child of God. I was created by God to live for God.* What better goal can anyone have? You want to be free...truly free? Live for God and let Christ live through you. Christianity, after all, is the religion of the forgiven.

Free to Serve

***I**n those days there was no king in Israel: every man did that which was right in his own eyes.* (Judges 21:25) Those words were penned thousands of years ago but they could have been written today and been just as true. It does seem that everyone believes he/she has the freedom to do whatever. No guidelines...if it feels good, do it. Consequently, today we suffer just as the Israelites did back then.

The book of Judges records seven different times, over a period of 305 years, that the Israelites sinned, became servants to their conquerors, repented, asked God for help, after which He brought them back to where they willingly served Him again. In reading news today I often wonder if America is on the brink of being conquered, of losing our precious freedom.

In II Timothy 3:1-5 we also read another portion of scripture that sounds a lot like our news today. **This know also, that in the last days perilous times shall come. For men shall be lovers of their own selves, covetous, boasters, proud, blasphemers, disobedient to parents, unthankful, unholy, without natural affection, trucebreakers, false accusers, incontinent, fierce, despisers of those that are good. Traitors, heady, highminded, lovers of pleasures more than lovers of God; Having a form of godliness, but denying the power thereof: from such**

turn away.

Doesn't that sound familiar? How did this happen? How can we reverse the trend? After all, this is America, the land of the free. Everyone has a "right" to his or her own opinion. That's true but everyone doesn't have the "right" to do as he/she pleases. We are still a land of laws.

What exactly does "free" mean? If each one of us were "free" to do whatever we want, would that bring chaos or peacefulness? That's a no-brainer question since it gives no guideline to follow. Rules are necessary to keep anarchy at abeyance. Rules limit each of us of our total freedom. That also means that someone has to be in charge, which means there must be guidelines. Our Founding Fathers were wise in establishing one of the best systems of government because they recognized the desire for freedom but the need for direction as well. Why do you suppose people from all over the world want to come *into* America, leaving their homelands? For over 230 years, we have managed to enjoy a freedom that no other country has.

That freedom has now brought us to the brink of disaster because we've lost our firm foundation. We have become as little children, each demanding his way, not willing to think of what's best for all.

We are all born "free" but what if a baby had no one to care for him? His freedom would soon bring death. His "freedom" to do whatever he wants stifles him. He needs to be nourished and guided. Unfortunately, some children are not receiving either the nourishment or guidance needed. We see turmoil and tragedy every day.

Every once in awhile a TV show comes along that truly instructs and makes sense. Such a show is *Nanny 911*. I have been amazed, and appalled, to see how ill prepared some educated parents are in taking charge of their children. It takes the Nanny a week to teach them and their children how to bring chaotic conditions into tranquil ones. How intelligent adults can be so ignorant about the basic fact that they are there to guide and direct their children instead of allowing the children to be in control never ceases to frustrate me.

Comedians have a field day with jokes about women wanting their way about everything and about hen-pecked spouses. And, we laugh but sometimes there's more truth than fiction to such tales. That is not the way God intended families to operate. Nor did he intend for women to be slaves to their spouse. God has always planned for a happy balance in nature as well as in humans. If He didn't plan for the sun, moon, stars and tides to be precise, we would burn up, freeze to death or be drowned. Our world was created by Intelligence. Certainly, the intricacies of our own bodies required more intelligence than that possessed by any human.

At the same time, every human being is created with freewill. What a gift that is! When one realizes that, it's easy to exercise that gift when we look to the One Who created everything in the beginning and guided by His power and love. Man's way has never worked. What better Guide can we have than the Creator Himself?

Giving Up

W*ives, be subject to your own husbands, as to the Lord.* (Ephesians 5:22) If you want to get the ire of a feminist, just quote that verse from the Bible. It does no good to tell her of a later verse that tells the husband to love his wife **just as Christ also loved the church**. A friend told me once that she didn't like Paul's writings because of what he said about women. I asked, "But, don't you believe that all scripture was written at the direction of the Holy Spirit?" She didn't. She preferred to pick and choose the parts of scripture that fit her beliefs. A lot of people are like that. They only want to accept certain passages with which they agree.

Being submissive isn't easy, especially for a strong-willed person. We've all seen a young child who believes he is capable of doing everything for himself no matter how difficult. He may end up making a mess of things but that's the way he learns. Parents are there to guide and nurture and still give the child free reign to grow.

God has provided us with a textbook to deal with all phases of life. Problems arise when we refuse to follow His instructions. In a devotional booklet telling about King Ahaz, it states he proceeded on his own course time and again even though God tried to turn his heart. Finally, only one question remained: How long will God's patience continue with His rebellious people?

From the beginning of recorded history of mankind, God has tried to keep his people on course. Yet, they have chosen to go their own way, getting deeper in trouble. In the Bible sometimes they did turn around and trust Him.

As I reread the devotional about King Ahaz and the question asked, I couldn't help but wonder if America is not at that crossroads now. God and especially Christians are demeaned through art, humor, education and just about every aspect of our lives. Yet, we are expected to remain "tolerant" while our values are trampled and the devil's values are lifted up as "normal."

I wonder: How long will God's patience continue with His rebellious people now before He says, "Enough already?" Or, will we give up, surrender and let God take over? A wife may never "submit" to her husband but unless we submit to the Lord, we're lost. As the famous hymn states: *"Trust and obey for there's no other way to be happy in Jesus but to trust and obey."*

Growing in Grace

When thinking of "growth" many pictures come to mind. A baby is born and the parents and doting grandparents look for continual growth. Photos are taken for posterity and records kept of the exact day the first tooth appears, first word spoken, etc. It is truly a joyous time. Today we have home gardeners, growing their own organic foods. Once the seed is planted, every day a check is made to see the first sprout spring forth. Each succeeding day the continuing growth is observed. Those who are fortunate enough to have finances to invest spend time watching the market on its rollercoaster ride.

The most amazing growth, however, comes when a person becomes a "new creature" because he accepts Christ as his Savior. Some take time over years to grow in the Spirit; others leap into full-blown stewardship of service immediately. Sometimes the road to Christian maturity is a bumpy one with hills and valleys along the way.

Some of our favorite hymns were penned by people who came to Christ with broken hearts. John Newton, who wrote the beloved *Amazing Grace*, was such a person. He was just 23 years old and already a sea captain, having begun his seafaring with his father at age 11, when he turned to Christ. During a violent storm it appeared his ship, crew and the African slave cargo would be lost. He cried out, "Lord, have mercy upon us." Afterwards in his cabin, he reflected upon those words as he had not had any religious training except for a short time as a youngster before his mother died. He gave his heart to Christ there in his cabin. He forsook his sea career and began studying at night. Sixteen years later, he was ordained a minister and spent the rest of his life preaching the gospel.

Another favorite hymn is *Wonderful Grace of Jesus*, written by Haldor Lillenas. He seemed destined to use his God-given musical talent to serve Christ. In this stirring hymn, he writes about the "matchless Grace of Jesus" and the fact there is nothing with which to compare it.

When we accept the gift of Christ through God's Grace, we have all that's needed to live and grow as a Christian. **"For by grace you have been saved through faith; and that not of yourselves, it is the gift of God."** (Ephesians 2:8) Too often people are willing to accept the gift but fail to use it. Just as water that doesn't flow becomes stagnate, Christians who don't use God's gift will too. Pure joy comes when we are growing in God's Grace.

Growing Up, Not Out

When we hear the phrase, "acting like a 2-year-old", we immediately envision a screaming, tantrum-throwing child. Right? Many parents express more than once during a child's two-year period that, "I'll sure be glad when this kid reaches three!" That's because even a loving parent doesn't appreciate such actions, let alone an onlooker.

It has jokingly been said there are five stages of life: Growing up, growing out, slimming down, holding it in, and finally, forget it. Sadly, that's about it for far too many people who go through life. Because the bad news dominates the media, we don't often hear about those who are making a difference and leaving their good mark on the world.

A friend and I stopped at a fast food place for a bite of lunch and in came a 30-something lady, all smiles, with six youngsters, most of whom were under five years of age. While the lady was ordering their meals, the oldest child, a girl who appeared to be about seven years old, guided the other two girls and three boys to a table and got them all seated. Talk about maturity! She was a real grown up in her actions. The children were all well-behaved and when they left, a man in the booth next to us remarked, "What a great bunch of kids!" We agreed. Whether all the children belonged to the lady or not, we knew that some were hers because they called her Mama. What a blessing to watch such a scene.

The Bible doesn't give us much information about Christ in his younger years. He was born; he was 12; and **He increased in wisdom and stature and in favor with God and man**. We are also told he worked with Joseph in his carpenter shop, thus he became known as The Carpenter. We know he was the eldest child among his siblings and it wasn't until after his resurrection they accepted him as their Savior. Most of what we know about Jesus is what he did after he was 30 years old.

In the New Testament God left it up to the Apostle Paul, a man without a family of his own according to tradition, to write down the instructions for Christians on how to raise their children. In Deuteronomy 6:7, God was very specific on what parents should do when He said, **And thou shall teach them diligently unto thy children, and shall talk of them when thou sittest in thine house, and when thou walkest by the way, and when thou liest down, and when thou risest up**. The "them" referred to herein are the commandments He had given the Israelites to follow. Each generation was to pass along those laws.

It seems to me that may be one reason we are inundated with so much evil news and activities today. Many parents no longer take the time to teach the precepts of God's commandments to their children. Even those who do are bucking a society filled with every kind of debauchery on all levels.

The older I get the more I realize that chronological age has nothing whatsoever to do with whether or not a person is mature. That's not to say one shouldn't become mature as the years add up. After all, life itself brings experiences that sometimes adds wisdom, but not always. "We learn from our mistakes," is a common phrase. It just takes more mistakes and more experience before some of us really learn! And, unless or until we learn, we don't mature.

After the 9/11/01 tragedies, Billy Graham's daughter Ann was asked, "Where was God? Why would a loving God allow such a thing to happen?" She gave the perfect answers. She reiterated how God had not forsaken America but rather Americans had forsaken Him. She said we stood by while the Bible and prayer were removed from our schools; discipline was no longer allowed in schoolrooms; free condoms were given to boys because "boys will be boys"; killing of babies (abortion) became acceptable; Internet pedophilia rose; bad language was overlooked; the entertainment industry corrupted our morals; leaders of our country openly cheated; and Dr. Spock's writings were adhered to instead of the Bible. We now know he finally admitted his ways were erroneous before he breathed his last breath but the damage was done.

We became a do-your-own-thing-if-it-feels-good society. No one seems willing to accept responsibility for his/her actions. Trial lawyers are having a field day with lawsuits because some people couldn't quit smoking or leave fattening fast food alone. It's sort of like the situation which occurred among the Israelites a thousand years ago. The last verse in the book of Judges states, **every man did that which was right in his own eyes**. For 350 years God came to their rescue when they repented and asked for His help. Years later the mighty Roman Empire collapsed after 422 years because of the degradation within.

Abraham Lincoln warned our young nation that, if we ever failed, it would be caused by corruption from within our borders. The communists knew that and attacked us by denigrating our educational system as one of their top priorities. In 1960 I attended an anti-communism rally in Los Angeles. One of the speakers was Karl Prussion who had been infiltrating churches as a communist youth worker. After becoming disillusioned he worked as a counterspy for the FBI. Pretty scary when we see what's happening today, 400 years since the pilgrims landed.

I wonder, are there enough God-fearing Americans left to turn this country around? Or, are we so self-centered and immature that we just don't care anymore? It's way past time to grow up, to throw off our 2-year-old attitudes and actions. It's time for Christians who do believe that God will rescue us, *if we repent*, put on the full armor of God and quit sitting back watching our world fall apart.

Be not deceived; God is not mocked: for whatsoever a man sows, that shall he also reap. (Galatians 6:9 KJV)

Honesty IS The Best Policy

"Honest and hope to die" was an off-repeated phrase among children when I was growing up. Or, while crossing our heart we'd say, "Cross my heart and hope to die!" Obviously, no child really "hopes to die" but with sincere emphasis that we meant what we said, we never thought through what we were saying. Unfortunately, some adults still do not think of the consequences when they are dishonest. In today's world dishonesty seems to be par for the course...the accepted thing. If you can get away with it, so be it.

In Proverbs 6:16-19 we read about the **six things the Lord hates, seven that are detestable to him: haughty eyes, a lying tongue, hands that shed innocent blood, a heart that devises wicked schemes, feet that are quick to rush into evil, a false witness who pours out lies and a man who stirs up dissension among brothers.** Let's look at each one.

First, **"haughty eyes."** Haughty means disdain or proud and more than once in God's Word we are warned about pride. It is not honest to think we are better than anyone else.

"A lying tongue" needs no explanation. What causes a person to lie about something? We have seen what happens to people at the top tumble because they were untruthful in their dealings with others. Not a good way to get ahead certainly.

"Hands that shed innocent blood" makes me think of those who practice abortion. It is beyond my comprehension how anyone could sanction that, especially partial birth abortion. At the time of this writing, there was a prisoner put to death by lethal injection. There is an incomparable difference between the taking of an innocent life and someone who is guilty of murder and paying the penalty for his unlawful acts.

"A heart that devises wicked schemes." When I hear about some of the schemes devised by some people's minds, I think how sad that they didn't use that innate talent for good. Evidently, some of the cleverest criminals have had high IQs. It's an adrenaline rush for them to deceive others, so they say.

"Feet that are quick to rush into evil." Haven't we all been drawn to something we knew in our hearts was not good for us...and still we yielded to the temptation? We are not being honest to ourselves when we fail to listen to our inner self.

"A false witness who pours out lies" seems to be prominent in our courts and in every day life any more. We see this all the time in the political realm. If a rumor is repeated often enough, people believe it is true. Or, how many times has a politician lost because at the last minute some untruth is spread and it's too late to refute it?

Finally, the Lord detests **"a man** (or woman) **who stirs up dissension among brothers."** In other words, DO NOT GOSSIP! Years ago I heard a sermon about the value of the spoken word. The pastor said we should be ever so careful about what we say out loud because once spoken it's impossible to retrieve every word. He said it's like opening a feather pillow and then trying to find every feather to put back in the case. Can't be done and the same is true about words. There are some who honestly don't realize the error of their way. They are simply passing along "news." There are others who deliberately relate some piece of "news" they know is false with the purpose of destroying the party of whom they speak.

One of my favorite verses in the Bible is found in Philippians 4:8. Paul has written to the Philippians that they should not worry about anything but to pray about everything. If they do, *the peace of God which passeth all understanding... through Jesus Christ* will be theirs. Then, he goes on, *Finally, brethren, whatsoever things are true, whatsoever things are honest, whatsoever things are just, whatsoever things are pure, whatsoever things are lovely, whatsoever things are of good report; if there be any virtue, and if there be any praise, think on these things.*

I Am Sorry

There are three words in the English language that seem to be the hardest to say for a lot of people. They are "I am sorry." If they were spoken more often, a lot of heartache and misunderstanding could be prevented. Of course, there are some humans who are the exception and saying, "I am sorry" comes easy for them.

I had a friend who would say, "I'm sorry" when she had nothing for which to be sorry. She simply didn't like conflict and this was her way of quickly settling a dispute. On the other hand, I've known people who would never utter, "I'm sorry" even when they were obviously in the wrong. Thus, turmoil festered and nothing was settled.

Think back to when you were a child and your mother told you to say you were sorry. The problem was, you weren't sorry...at least, not always. When I became a mother, I trained my son the same way. He probably thought the same as I.

But, if you aren't the one in the wrong, should you be willing to end an argument by saying, "I'm sorry"? That's where Christ's teachings about going the extra mile, turning your cheek or giving up your cloak comes in and that's hard...really hard! Even when Christ was innocent of any sin and was being crucified, he asked God to forgive his murderers because,

They know not what they do. (Luke 23:34)

Sometimes I tune into one of the popular TV shows that present human tragedy stories. Once I heard three people tell of devastating events in their lives. In every case, they related that they would never forgive themselves for their mistake. How sad. The Bible clearly tells us that there is only one sin for which we cannot be forgiven. In Matthew 12:31 we read, **Wherefore I say unto you, All manner of sin and blasphemy shall be forgiven unto men: but the blasphemy against the Holy Ghost shall not be forgiven unto men.** In other words, unless we refuse to accept the gift of Christ, we can be forgiven of anything...*if* we confess our sin and repent!

The 15-year-old girl had been seduced at age 13 by an older man who had children her age. She believed he loved her and she *knew* she loved him. Now she realizes how foolish she was.

A young man was illegally drag racing and ended up crashing into another car. When he looked through the windshield, there lay his mother, dead. Sorry? He's more than sorry. He will never forget the accident and how foolish he was and he believes he will never forgive himself.

A young mother didn't take the time to buckle her little daughter in a car seat. When their truck was in an accident, she and her two children were thrown out of the car. She was not hurt but her two children had been thrown to the pavement below. Her son lived but not her baby daughter. She is tormented with the memory and unable to forgive herself.

All of these people were telling their stories as warning to others who might make the same mistakes. For that reason they can be commended. But, their stories shouldn't end there.

I have never met a person who is perfect. Every one of us has sinned in some way either in sins of commission or sins of omission. The apostle Paul even admitted, **For the good that I would I do not; but the evil which I would not, that I do.** (Romans 7:19) He realized he was a sinner just like everyone else. Further on in verses 24 and 25 he wrote, **O wretched man that I am! Who shall deliver me from the body of this death? I thank God through Jesus Christ our Lord. So then with the mind I myself serve the law of God; but with the flesh the law of sin.**

King David was definitely a man who sinned in just about every way possible, including adultery and murder. Yet, when he repented, he penned one of the most heart-rending psalms in the Bible. In Psalm 51 he pleads, **Have mercy upon me, O God, according to thy lovingkindness; according unto the multitude of thy tender mercies blot out my transgressions. Wash me thoroughly from mine iniquity, and cleanse me from my sin. For I acknowledge my transgressions: and my sin is ever before me. Against thee, thee** *only, have I sinned and done this evil in thy sight: that thou mightest be justified when thou speakest, and be clear when thou judgest.* Once he acknowledged his sin, he willingly repented and pled to God for forgiveness.

There is a way "out" for everyone. It comes down to whether we want to admit our sins and say "I'm sorry" with true repentance. It is then that we will be free from the bondage of sin. On the day of Pentecost the people asked Peter what they should do to be saved. He responded, *Repent, and be baptized every one of you in the name of Jesus Christ for the remission of sins, and ye shall receive the gift of the Holy Ghost.* (Acts 2:38)

Do you want "peace like a river"? Then practice saying "I am sorry" to those you offend and especially to God, the Only One, who is able to give you that kind of peace.

Joyful Living

She's the most beautiful baby I've ever seen I thought as I looked through the nursery window and saw my first grandchild. Tears of joy ran down my cheeks as I stood mesmerized looking at her. Although she's grown into a beautiful young lady now, I had to confess later when I saw her newborn picture that she probably wasn't as pretty as my eyes first told me. Beauty is in the eye of the beholder!

Centuries ago another babe was born who was beautiful beyond description whose purpose in coming was to bring more joy to the world than anyone could have imagined. Why? Because His birth manifested pure love which in turn brings pure joy to mankind. The angels proclaimed this fact. The shepherds stood in awe at the reality of it. And the wise men proved their wisdom by their actions.

Just as today, there were people then who didn't accept God's Gift and tried to destroy Him. Down through the ages, man has continued to go against God and what has it caused? Certainly not joy! When people accept God's Son, what a difference it makes, not only in their own life but also in the lives of others around them. Jesus came to bring "Peace on Earth" even though some will not accept it. Therefore, we continue to have wars and rumors of war.

Learning this issue of *The Christian Journal*

was to have the theme of "Joy" brought to mind several scriptures from the Old Testament as well as the New Testament: **_Joy cometh in the morning; Make a joyful noise unto God; Enter into the joy of thy salvation; Be glad also with exceeding joy._** In one Bible concordance I counted 67 verses referring to 'joy', 'joyful' or 'joyous'. God must have intended for us to experience that wonderful feeling.

Many times, we read in the Bible where 'joy' follows a sorrow or chastisement. King David was a "man after God's own heart," yet he was a murderer and an adulterer! When he bowed down in true repentance and faced his sins, God healed him and David then wrote many of the psalms that speak of joy. Isn't that true in our lives as well? We may not be guilty of murder or adultery, but every one of us is guilty of some sin at sometime for there was only One Perfect Person...Christ, our Lord. In order to have the fulfillment of joy, we must repent of any sin.

"Ha," you might say, "I know lots of people who don't know Christ as Savior who are happy and enjoying life. What about them?"

I, too, know, and love, people who do not know Christ and appear to be very satisfied with their life. The kind of joy, and/or happiness, they have is NOT the true joy that ONLY comes from God. It is impossible to have pure joy apart from God just as it is impossible to know true love without God. God IS love! Any other type of love is human based.

I marvel at, and regret, the number of times God has had to pick me up after I have willfully gone my own way, doing things MY way! Yet, He's been there, ready to give me a hand, oftentimes through friends who see me suffer. How thankful I am for those times when I come face to face with my own inadequacies and have to turn back to God for help. The joy that comes back then is greater than any joy known before.

More than one couple has said that the "making up" after a bitter quarrel makes their lives better than ever. We all go through valleys and back up to the mountaintops in this life. As Paul wrote, we now **see through a glass darkly** but eventually we will see Christ **face to face** (I Corinthians 13:12) when we reach eternity. That is when we will realize the promise of no more pain, nor sorrow...just pure joy.

A friend has written a book about her experiences of motherhood. She titled it, *"Refreshing Hope In God, A Mother's Journey of Joy and Pain."* Within the pages of her story, Judy Dippel reveals the depth of despair and the thrill of joy of being a mother. I dare say there are few parents who have not experienced both. Without pain, we can't really know what joy is, and vice versa.

The acronym J O Y is the best answer I know on how to find happiness. It stands for Jesus-Others-Yourself. Put Jesus first, Others second and Yourself last. **Seek ye first the kingdom of God and his righteousness, and all these**

things shall be added unto you, Matthew 6:33 tells us. It's when we get things out of order we run into problems.

"Joy to the world, the Lord has come!" We need to remember that when He came He brought with Him pure love and pure joy! Because of that, we win life's battles when we embrace Him!

Little Is Much

"Little is much when God is in it," the first line of a hymn, kept running through my mind as I listened to a native pastor from Kenya tell about the living conditions in his area. One lady observed that, "There's a difference between hunger and starvation. We have people who are hungry here in America, but we don't see the starvation because we have organizations to help them."

It reminded me of the slogan one of the ladies came up with at a recent missions meeting when she said, "Your change can change lives." We had been discussing how little it takes to feed a lot of people in countries such as Kenya, Haiti or Afghanistan. It's amazing how far $5 or $10 can go in some of those third world countries.

The story about how the Temple Baptist Church in Philadelphia was built is one that illustrates what God can do with very little. At the turn of the century a pastor befriended a poor little girl. After two years she died but in her effects an old worn out purse with 57 cents was found. On a slip of paper in childish handwriting she had written that she was saving so a larger building could be built and there would be room for more children to attend Sunday School. When her story became known through the newspaper, God instilled in the hearts of first one person with means to many more. The 57 cents snowballed until the 3,300 seat Temple Baptist Church, Temple University and the Good Samaritan Hospital became realities. All because one little girl wanted others to learn about Jesus.

It amazes me how foreigners come here and learn the English language so readily when we have many words that are spelled the same way but with different meanings. One word in particular has been overused and misused. That word is love. "I love my car... dog... bike... house...suit...wife...husband....child....mother.... father...kitchen." You get the idea. We flippantly toss out that precious word, making it almost meaningless. February could be called the Love Month because of Valentine's Day when cards are sent that are either humorous or sentimental.

Actually, December is the true Love Month because that's when we remember that **God so loved the world that He gave His only begotten Son.** The Greeks used different words for love. Their 'agape' kind of love in John 3:16 tells us precisely how deeply God cared for us. He took pity on us but more than that, He had mercy for us to the point that He gave His Son so we might have eternal life. The fact that Christ was willingly obedient to His Father is something we should savor. That kind of love reveals *true* compassion.

Christ taught us to look at our fellow man

with compassion when He said, ***Inasmuch as ye have done it unto the least of these, my brethren, ye have done it unto me.*** (Matthew 25:40b) Nearly every missionary I've heard has said how important it is to first be a friend to those in need by feeding them food before trying to reach them with the gospel. Isn't that what Christ did? He fed the multitudes, getting their attention, then he preached to them. First the physical food followed by spiritual truths.

We don't have to travel far to see this type of compassion because The Salvation Army has demonstrated this kind of caring for the downtrodden since 1865 when it was organized in England by Gen. William Booth. For the first 13 years it was known as the Christmas Mission and then the name was changed to The Salvation Army at Christmas 1878. If it weren't for that organization, there would be many that would go hungry.

Many other such organizations, including churches, are abundant nowadays. They operate solely on support from private funds without government help or intervention. I am reminded of IDES (International Disaster Emergency Service), based in Indiana. Although it is a fundamental Christian group, they respond to every type of disaster anywhere in the world, not just here in the United States. They have been responsible for supplying food, clothing and shelter whenever and wherever needed, all in the name of Jesus Christ.

In a newsletter they told the story of a 10-year old boy walking along the seashore. He was picking up starfish that had washed ashore and throwing them back into the water. A man, coming down the beach and seeing what he was doing told him, "There are too many starfish. What you are doing won't make a difference." As the boy picked up another starfish and threw it into the water, he turned to the man and said, "It'll make a difference for that one."

Each one of us alone can't make much of a dent but working together, we can make a big difference. When I asked my friend Joshua from Kenya what their money was, he replied, "Shillings." I then asked how many shillings it would take to make one dollar. I was stunned when he said, "Eighty."

It is my firm belief that when we give with love and compassion God can take 80 shillings, or 57 cents, and work wonders because "Little *is* much when God is in it!"

Looking on the Inside

As I glanced down the aisle of the small plane looking for my seat, I saw him. He was noticeable because he looked so different from every other passenger. First of all, he was BIG! He had a full beard, long hair past his shoulders, wore a black, sleeveless T-shirt with a black leather vest over that and his arms were covered with tattoos. He looked exactly like a Hell's Angel. And guess what? He was sitting in the aisle seat next to the window seat assigned to me. *Oh no,* I thought. When I stopped and indicated I needed to get into the window seat, he graciously rose and stepped into the aisle, giving me plenty of room to get in.

I always carry reading material whenever I travel so I got my book out and began reading. As we headed south over the snow-capped mountains I remarked, "There's still quite a bit of snow on the mountains." He agreed and gradually we began a conversation.

He was headed for Washington, D.C. to participate with the motorcycle riders who were going to ride to honor our veterans over the Memorial Day weekend. "I'm going to rent a bike in Arlington for the two days I'll be there," he told me. He only wished his wife could have joined him because he was going to miss her. In fact, he said, "I rode over to my friend's last night from the coast and I already miss her." His voice was soft like a "Gentle Ben."

Hmmm, this fellow must be a "normal" person...not one of those Hell's Angels type.

He told me how he was extending his boat, which he used to capture crab, and proceeded to tell me how they now are able to do that. As we started our descent into San Francisco, he said, "The last time I was here, it took 36 hours because that's how long it took by boat."

The entire experience was most pleasant but the best part was when he talked about his wife and the Lord. Yes, the Lord! His wife is a counselor, helping people get off addictions and because she's been successful at it, she loves her job. "But," he said, "it's actually the Lord who helps them. That's what it takes for it to stick."

Wow! Shame on me! Because I was looking on the outside, I was holding back and left our encounter up to another to witness for the Lord!

I was so thankful for my seat companion on the first leg of my trip for I was reminded of what the Lord told Samuel in I Samuel 16:7 when he said, **The Lord does not look at the things man looks at. Man looks at the outward appearance, but the Lord looks at the heart.**

What a wonderful reminder! Confession is good for the soul.

Ministers for Christ

A few years ago on a Sunday night about 9:00 p.m. a relative phoned to ask me if I would call my pastor to go to the hospital because her husband was dying. They had not attended church and did not know a pastor who could offer comfort at such a time. I have to admit I hesitated, but not for judgmental reasons. I knew my pastor was totally exhausted because of a stressful weekend. In spite of that, I agreed to call him and he immediately responded.

His lack of self-concern and the love he showed her that night was very much appreciated. Not only by her, by it gave me a new appreciation for him. That incident is just one of many he endures every week, along with most pastors. The dedicated ones suffer heartache and fatigue all the time. It's part of their job. Because of that, and because they are human, many have fallen by the wayside. When Christians pray for their pastors, it's just one small way we can sustain them.

There are missionaries who are called to serve in far away places and oftentimes without the modern conveniences we take for granted. I marvel at the joy they relate when they have been able to help people because once they feed, clothe and offer medical care, they can preach the Good News of Christ. Missionaries know that a changed heart makes a world of difference in everyone's life, especially those who have so little of the world's amenities. In parts of Africa, former warriors have become evangelists for Christ.

One missionary family on furlough for several months stated they couldn't wait to return to Kenya even though living there was dangerous and didn't include a lot of comfort or conveniences. They have such a love for people who are without Christ, they were more than willing to give up everything here.

Years ago when I had to go to the hospital for an emergency, my doctor later asked me why I hadn't called him. I said, "It was the weekend and I hated to bother you." He let me know that he could be called any time. Today, doctors have others on call so they can get needed rest.

Here again, we have human beings who are being stretched to the utmost for physical and mental endurance. All those in the medical profession experience the entire gamut of human tragedy. It takes dedication with a heart for helping others to be true servants, willing to put aside their own desires to minister to others.

When my grandson visited his sister's first grade schoolroom he noticed one little boy who had been a problem all year, causing disruption nearly every day. After the visit Adam said, "They don't pay Andrea nearly enough!"

There has been talk about allowing teachers to carry guns to protect themselves from those few who insist on causing trouble. Nearly every week there is some breaking story about a tragedy in a school because some kid has gone berserk. Teaching school has become a hazardous profession. Yet, a dedicated teacher is willing to face such ordeals to minister an education to children.

Policemen's families send their loved ones off to work wondering if they will return home. Some don't. Because of a few bad apples in the profession, who get most of the attention, the majority of law officers who are good are not always given the accolades they deserve. The same is true of firemen who willingly put their lives on the line to help where and whenever needed. Did you know many firemen help with emergency medical care as much as they do putting out fires?

One cannot write about ministers, or ministering, without mentioning angels. In the Old Testament we find numerous sources of angels who were actually seen by and talked to people.

In chapter one of Hebrews, the writer relates how the Son is greater than the angels and in verses 13 and 14 we read, **But to which of the angels said he at any time, Sit on my right hand, until I make thine enemies thy footstool? Are they not all ministering spirits, sent forth to minister for them who shall be heirs of salvation?** In other words, we humans are more important to God than angels. They are ministering spirits who watch over and protect those who are saved.

Christ came to earth as a human. ***For verily he took not on him the nature of angels; but he took on him the seed of Abraham, Wherefore in all things it behooved him to be made like unto his brethren, that he might be a merciful and faithful high priest in things pertaining to God, to make reconciliation for the sins of the people. For in that he himself hath suffered being tempted, he is able to succor them that are tempted.*** (Hebrews 2:14-18)

In Mark 10:45 we read why Christ came. ***For even the Son of man came not to be ministered unto, but to minister, and to give his life a ransom for many.***

One does not have to have a particular job, such as minister, doctor, teacher, policeman or fireman to minister to others. Every Christian should be ministering to others. ***Do unto others as you would have others do unto you*** (Matthew 7:12) is a basic Bible teaching. Those who live by it find peace and contentment, especially those who do good in the name of Jesus Christ.

No Man Is An Island

No Man Is An Island is the title of a famous meditation by English Clergyman John Donne (1572-1631). He wrote it during the Renaissance period. When I think of fellowship, I think of how important it is to a human life and so I decided to read about this poem in order to understand what Donne's thinking was behind it. This particular work brings out two thoughts: mankind is interconnected and mankind's mortality.

My thinking and Donne's are in complete agreement that God is the Creator of all mankind, thus we are all interconnected. When one of us hurts, we hurt with him/her. We have a common bond in that regard. When someone dies, we grieve with the family. Donne ends with the thought that none of us knows when the bell with toll for us.

Recently in a week's time, our church suffered the loss of a dear brother in Christ. No sooner had we heard of his death than we learned two elders lost their mothers and another member's brother had been found dead in his home. Three of the deaths were expected because of their age and circumstances. The latter one was a shock.

That is when the fellowship of the brotherhood in congregations comes together to offer love, understanding and support. That's exactly what we all did...family and friends. None of us within ourselves has the strength to bear the burden of so many losses. But, we know the One Who does! What a difference it makes!

There is another type of fellowship known to all people everywhere no matter race, creed or gender. Whenever we get together with like-minded friends and relatives, there's a bond...a warm feeling one for the other. Almost everyone has experienced that kind of fellowship, even the heathens in faraway places. That's a part of human nature. To repeat, *No man is an island*.

Of course there are, and have always been, those individuals who prefer to be alone. How sad. They don't know what they're missing. I've often wondered if some of them have become hermits because at one time they were deeply hurt and decided they never wanted to go through that kind of hurt again.

Others become isolated when a spouse dies and they don't know how to reach out to other people. It takes an effort to make a new life. I can attest to that. If someone is naturally shy, it takes even more effort. For seniors who are left alone after years of marriage, there is no need not to become involved with others. Local Senior Centers offer something of interest to any person, no matter what his/her interest may be. There are various service-type clubs all over. If someone has a mind to volunteer, there is no limit of places needing help.

As a youth, my parents constantly reminded me how important good friends were. Peer pressure is something all young people go through on their way to adulthood. I attended a seminar about methamphetamine and the troubles it brings to society. Not having any young people around for several years, what I heard was an eye-opener. I had no idea that most of the crime is caused by people addicted to meth. That includes child abuse. I sat next to a young man who told me, "I became addicted at age 7." "Seven?" I asked him. "Were your parents drug addicts?" "No, they were never addicts. I just got into it with friends." Thankfully, he had been "clean" for 18 months.

Because of my parents' counsel, I didn't get into *too* much trouble and now my own choice for fellowship is mostly the church. Not only do I find fellowship with others, but my spiritual values are renewed. There's a praise hymn, *I'm so glad I'm a part of the family of God* by Bill and Gloria Gaither that fits this idea perfectly. For someone who is without nearby blood relatives, there is no better "family" than *The Family of God.*

In Galatians 6:2 we are admonished to **Bear ye one another's burdens, and so fulfill the law of Christ.** That is what happens when Christians suffer loss. The Body of Christ rallies around them. They realize they are not alone. *Am I my brother's keeper?* asked Cain. The answer to all of us is, "Yes." God created us to care for and love one another. Christ Himself gave this command in John 15:12: ***This is my commandment, That ye love one another, as I have loved you.***

On the other hand, we are instructed in Ephesians 5:11 to ***have no fellowship with the unfruitful works of darkness, but rather reprove them***. Some people absolutely reject anything to do with Christ and His Father. That does not mean we are to reject them. We are to love and pray for them with all fervor. I've heard many stories from people who once walked in sin and darkness and turned their lives around once they came to know Christ. ***With God, all things are possible,*** according to Matthew 10:27. As long as there is breath, there is hope for better things to come. As Christians, we should pattern our lives after the first Christians who ***continued steadfastly in the apostles' doctrine and fellowship, and in breaking of bread, and in prayers.*** (Acts 2:42)

It's true, *No man is an island*. In Donne's dissertation of his piece he wrote, *I take mine own into contemplation* (speaking of sickness) *and so secure myself by making my recourse to God, who is our only security*. God is our only security. In Hebrews 9:27 we read there is no second chance. ***And as it is appointed unto men once to die, but after this the judgment.***

Better to have fellowship with others who are like-minded because none of us is an island nor do we know when the bell will toll... *for us.*

No One is Pure...But

B**lessed are the pure in heart, for they shall see God.** (Matthew 5:8) What a promise that Beatitude is! Yet, I ask myself, "Is there anyone who is truly 'pure in heart" in this day and age? Too many seem to have a spirit of taking all they can and getting it any way they can.

One of the saddest stories in the entire Bible is the one about David and Bathsheba. Because of the movie industry, nearly everyone is familiar with the story... up to a point. David saw; he wanted; he conquered. But then, he suffered. David compounded his sin further by causing murder. When Nathan comforted him of his sin, David confessed and asked forgiveness from God. Hence, one of the most beautiful verses in the Bible: **Create in me a clean heart, O God; and renew a right spirit within me.** (Psalm 51:10)

My pastor, Dr. Aaron Veach, gave a series of sermons on "Extreme Makeover," a take-off of the TV show but with a very different perspective. The last one dealt with the whole idea of purity. He offered four truths:
1. I can please God by how I live! Or, I can offend God by how I live!
2. I am called to live a holy life!
3. I will be judged for my sins! We keep them until we specifically confess them.

4. I have the Holy Spirit to help me!

He went on to say, "We feed both pure and impure motives. We need to feed the desires that lead us to God and to starve the evil desires." He listed some things we could do to promote purity, such as pursuing Godly thoughts; avoiding tempting situations; controlling visual desires; confessing wrongs; and maintaining a one-on-one mind set with God and with another human being in accountability.

"God wants us to know he loves each one of us individually. God doesn't just love the whole world; but he loves the individual, each and every one of us! Accountability helps hold us to purity. It is much more difficult to sin if we know someone else will know what we are doing and not approve!" he concluded.

It might be easier to obey if we stop to remember that no matter where we are, God sees us. ***Whither shall I go from thy spirit? Or whither shall I flee from thy presence? If I ascend up into heaven, thou art there; if I make my bed in hell, behold, thou art there.*** Psalm 139:7, 8)

The Apostle Paul also gave some good advice. ***Finally, brethren, whatsoever things are true, whatsoever things are honest, whatsoever things are just, whatsoever things are pure, whatsoever things are lovely, whatsoever things are of good report; if there be any virtue, and if there be any praise, think on these things.*** (Philippians 4:8)

Obedience to God's Will

Years ago we played a get-acquainted parlor game. While sitting in a circle, the first person introduced himself with an adjective that began with the same letter as his first name such as Cheerful Charlie. The next person had to repeat that name and then give an example of his own. It was fun, and made it easier to remember names. When it came my turn, I used the adjective "Willful" and heard several "Amens!"

When I was 35 years old we learned our only child had developed some kind of a heart problem. I turned completely to God. My peace of mind came when I prayed, "Thy will be done, and God, whatever that is, help us accept it."

People have said, "Well, how can I know God's will?" The best way is to read the Bible, which is his inspired instruction book. I'm guilty of trying to put something together without checking the instructions. I usually go back to, "When all else fails, read the instructions." Works every time!

The Bible is filled with directions on how to live in accordance to God's Will. Although I advocate church attendance and listening to the Word in song, prayer and preaching, I also believe that people have come to know Christ just by reading his Word.

"But it's so hard to understand," some say and give up. I doubt if there has ever been or ever will be any human who fully understands all the wisdom in the Bible. But, there is enough that is very simple and easy to comprehend. Besides, there are verses which tell us how much God loves us, **For God so loved the world he gave us his only begotten Son that whosoever believeth in him should not perish but have everlasting life. For God sent not his Son into the world to condemn the world; but that the world through him might be saved.** (John 3:16-17)

The Bible also gives guidance for what not to do. ***It is God's will that you should be holy; that you should avoid sexual immorality; that each of you should learn to control his own body in a way that is holy and honorable, not in passionate lust like the heathen, who do not know God; and that in this matter no one should wrong his brother or take advantage of him. The Lord will punish men for all such sins, as we have already told you and warned you. For God did not call us to be impure, but to live a holy life. Therefore, he who rejects this instruction does not reject man but God, who gives you his Holy Spirit.*** (I Thessalonians 4:3-8 NIV) Think about it. Every type of entertainment today ignores those words.

Now, I've given up the adjective "Willful" for "Willing," a servant ready, willing and able to do God's Will.

Peaceful Harmony

I gnorance is bliss," my grandpa said more than once, explaining that people who didn't know what is going on in the world were the happiest. He'd add, *"That's why people who don't have much to worry about are happy."* Now that we have instant communication, not only in the world but also from outer space, there's not much that happens we don't hear about within seconds. It's hard to remain ignorant if one watches the news at all.

When a disaster takes place in any part of the world we see the devastation and our hearts empathize with those experiencing the event. Within hours help is pouring in from people and governments to alleviate the suffering.

So, why is it there is bitterness and hatred in the world? In the Bible James wrote: **What causes fights and quarrels among you? Don't they come from your desires that battle within you? You want something but don't get it. You kill and covet, but you cannot have what you want. You quarrel and fight. You do not have, because you do not ask God. When you ask, you do not receive because you ask with wrong motives, that you may spend what you get on your pleasures. You adulterous people, don't you know that friendship with the world is hatred toward God? Anyone who chooses to** *be a friend of the world becomes an enemy of God*. (NIV James 1:1-4) Wow! That's pretty clear and those statements apply to individuals and families as well as governments.

We are not left without a solution on how to obtain peace and harmony. James further wrote, *Submit yourselves, then, to God. Resist the devil, and he will flee from you. Come near to God and he will come near to you*. (NIV James 1:7-8)

I like to read western novels for one reason: it's easy to tell who the good guys are from the bad ones and the good guys always win! It would be nice if that were true in real life. Sometimes the good guys don't win; at least, not in this life. The Bible gives us several illustrations of people who suffered unjustly. In Genesis we read about Joseph who was sold and imprisoned although he was faultless. Innocent Daniel was thrown into the lion's den but was saved because God protected him.

The best example of one who was tortured and wrongly accused is Christ Himself. The only perfect man who ever existed died for everyone else's sin. We can have perfect peace of mind, if not in this lifetime, then in eternity because He arose from the grave and conquered death! As the hymnist wrote *Hallelujah! What a Savior!*

Reason or Excuses

"Are you alright?" my friend asked when she called. "I'm fine. Why?" "I thought you were going to stop by today." "No. Tomorrow on my way to church for the Christmas Party." "That was today," she said. "Today? Is today Thursday?" "It sure is," she replied.

Well, I missed a good fun-filled party because I forgot what day it was. I've heard that happens when people retire but it was the first time it happened to me. One day melts into another. That was my reason, my excuse, for being absent and we've laughed about it since. No harm was done, fortunately.

A minister told me that he once forgot to go to a funeral service where he was to be in charge. Now that wasn't a laughing matter at the time. The fact is we are all human and "things" happen, some of which we can control and others over which we can't.

Since 9-11 we've all heard about people who were saved from a horrible death because of some quirky incident that came up that morning. What was a minor irritation at the time proved to be forever imprinted on their minds as they think of the "what if" that might have been.

What about traffic snarls that cause people to be late for appointments? Or, worse yet, having an accident that causes someone to miss a meeting altogether? Some things are unforeseen and some aren't. If a person abuses his body with food and/or drink, there are consequences. If a person never exercises, there's a reason the body deteriorates. There's a reason behind every mishap or unfortunate trial in our life.

There is no better reason for reading and studying the Bible than the one Peter wrote in I Peter 3:15. ***Always be prepared to give an answer to everyone who asks you to give the reason for the hope that you have. But do this with gentleness and respect***.

The Bible is so full of knowledge, there is no way any human can ever understand all its wisdom. Not ever reading it, however, is a good way of insuring oneself of never learning the truth within. If we say we are a Christian, we should be able to share our faith with others. What better way to learn than to read the instruction Book God provided. He even sent the Holy Spirit to guide and to help us. We're not alone; therefore, we have no reason or excuse not to know His Will for us. How about making daily Bible reading a New Year's resolution?

Reconciliation with Christ

Before computers, it wasn't always easy to balance a checkbook. Now, in a matter of minutes, the task is finished and I find another reason to thank the Lord. If only our lives could be reconciled after turmoil as conveniently and quickly, what a difference life would be.

It doesn't matter how much we give if we cannot forgive. In Matthew 5:24 during the Sermon of the Mount, Christ said, ***...if you are offering your gift at the altar and there remember that your brother has something against you, leave your gift there in front of the altar. <u>First</u> go and be reconciled to your brother; <u>then</u> come and offer your gift.*** That is difficult, especially if we were the one who was hurt by someone's actions or words.

Anyone who has ever taken care of an elderly parent or loved one who is no longer in his/her right mind has probably experienced many times when something hurtful was said. We have to believe the person isn't aware of what is said. The disease of Alzheimer has been devastating to families.

After a parent loses a child through a tragedy, (a drunk driver or pedophile), it takes more than human understanding to forgive the perpetrator. Some people can't and end up suffering themselves. Others find release for their own spirit by forgiving and praying for the guilty party.

It's only through God's grace and His willingness to sacrifice His Son that we can be reconciled to Him. **We are therefore Christ's ambassadors, as though God were making his appeal through us. We implore you on Christ's behalf: Be reconciled to God. God made him who had no sin to be sin for us, so that in him we might become the righteousness of God.** (II Corinthians 5:20,21)

Aside from Christ Himself, there's never been a perfect person. More than once the scriptures tell us that **There is none righteous, no, not one** (Romans 3:10)

Are you troubled, worried, fretting, angry, frustrated, heartsick? **Cast all your anxiety on him because he cares for you.** (I Peter 5:7)

Refreshing Entertainment

This year I did something I hadn't done in years. I watched the Academy Awards. I had seen the film *The Blind Side* and was interested in how it might fare. Pleasantly surprised, it won several accolades. Based on a true story involving a Christian family, that seemed almost unheard of in this day and age.

In recent years we have been inundated with books, films, magazines and every kind of entertainment there is that deals with the seamy side of life. Because of that, many believe we are in the "last days." Everywhere we turn, we hear of hatred and destruction. Over 2000 years ago the apostle Paul foretold what it will be like in the last days as recorded in 2 Timothy 3:1-5. ***But mark this: There will be terrible times in the last days. People will be lovers of themselves, lovers of money, boastful, proud, abusive, disobedient to their parents, ungrateful, unholy, without love, unforgiving, slanderous without self-control, brutal, not lovers of the good, treacherous, rash, conceited, lovers of pleasure rather than lovers of God...having a form of godliness but denying its power. Have nothing to do with them.***

Those words certainly apply today. America hit the slippery slope when abortion was legalized and we have picked up speed since.

Whereas politicians used to be regarded with

high esteem, they have sunk to a new low. Christians should know what a candidate believes and vote for those who espouse their values.

"Garbage in, garbage out" aptly applies to our choice of entertainment. Many sex offenders have admitted to being addicted to pornography. But, there is hope. Just as there have been some worthwhile films recently, as a reader, I'm delighted there are Christian authors. They write about people who overcome their heartaches and survive. One such author locally is Karen Ball. Her characters come alive and portray thoughts and anxieties almost everyone experiences. Without being preachy, she incorporates scripture to solve problems.

It is refreshing to be able to sit down and enjoy a good story without having to skip over four-letter words and explicit scenes better left to one's imagination. There are many fine Christian authors surfacing and they deserve our support.

Revealed Truth

Who hasn't learned from hindsight as events in our lives unfold? If only we had used better judgment, the consequences of our actions might have been easier to accept. People learn by asking questions and by making mistakes. Learning by the latter method seems to stick with us better. As humans we all make mistakes. Blessings come when we apply the new knowledge. In I Corinthians 13:12 Paul stated that, **Now we see but a poor reflection as in a mirror; then we shall see face to face.** For those who accept God's gift of His Son, Jesus Christ, there will come a time when the mysteries in this life will be revealed.

How can there be so many different religious beliefs in the world? Could it be that men follow other men's writings and interpretations rather than the inspired Word of God? True, God used humans to write the words of the Bible, and perhaps some discrepancies occurred along the way but God provided us an answer to that assumption. **Knowing this first, that no prophecy of the scripture is of any private interpretation. For the prophecy came not in old time by the will of man: but holy men of God spake as they were moved by the Holy Spirit.** (I Peter 1:20-21)

If one studies the entire Bible, it's easy to see there is a strain of truth in the inspired message that Jesus Christ was there at creation, that He came to earth as a man, that He died sinless to reconcile sinful man to God and that He rose from the grave and ascended back to heaven. There is no other human ever born who can claim such uniqueness.

In spite of any minor errors one might focus on in the Bible, there is a sustaining truth that cannot be denied. God is love and He desires all His creatures to come to Him. The preacher of Ecclesiastes ends with these words: ***Now all has been heard; here is the conclusion of the matter: Fear God and keep his commandment, for this is the whole duty of man. For God will bring every deed into judgment, including every hidden thing, whether it is good or evil.*** (Chapter 12:13-14)

One aspect that gives the Bible credence is the fact that all facets of the heroes/saints' lives are revealed. Godly men are shown to have weaknesses and yet God forgave them when they repented of their sins. We are given the same opportunity.

Setting Priorities

I was not just mad and angry, I was *FURIOUS!* How dare the monopoly cable company make such drastic changes without informing us ahead of time! And...to make changes which disrupt our TV viewing so totally! Unless we pay more, we have no 24/7 news stations. You bet I was angry. I wanted *my* news station.

Then, something happened. I received an email asking for prayer for one of the young mothers in our church. Why? Her ex-husband had taken his life, along with their 11-year-old son's. In my mind's eye I could see Zach running around, always smiling, full of life. He was her only child and as a mother of an only son, I wondered how she was going to cope with such a tragedy.

A week later I dreaded going to the memorial service but wanted to offer as much comfort as I could with my presence. The church was packed as friends joined relatives in remembering this vibrant boy. As one after another spoke about what Zach had meant to them, we laughed and cried. He certainly was "all boy" as they say. He had lived full speed ahead in his short 11 years, enjoying every minute. He knew how to love and let others know he loved them...never hesitating to give someone a big hug and tell them.

No one can truly understand the heartache of losing a child for whatever reason. Only those who have suffered that experience. Now a young mother was in that category.

Then I remembered the reassuring scripture in Philippians, chapter 4 wherein we read:

Be careful for nothing; but in every thing by prayer and supplication with thanksgiving let your requests be made known unto God. And the peace of God, which passeth all under-standing, shall keep your hearts and minds through Christ Jesus. I pray she will find comfort by doing that.

Her situation reminded me once again that there are far more serious events in life than losing cable television. What I had to get used to was nothing compared with what lay ahead for Laura. It didn't take long until I resolved my problem. Laura will be living with her heartache the rest of her life.

Simple Faith

As children we were taught the simple night time prayer *Now I lay me down to sleep. I pray the Lord my soul to keep. If I should die before I wake, I pray the Lord my soul to take.* Then, we would add a litany of supplications such as *God bless Mother and Daddy,* and continue naming brother, sister, grandparents, aunts, uncles, cousins, playmates and any pets we had. It was a simple routine, uttering a simple, basic belief in a Power greater than we.

Because of what is happening in our world today, children must not be taught that anymore and that's sad. They have no foundation. No security. No trust.

Now that I've reached the other end of the lifeline spectrum and know my time on this earth is shorter, I was thinking about that prayer. Simple as it is, it is comforting. Tragic and heart-rending as sudden death is, what a blessing for the one who is taken instantly into the arms of Jesus without having to endure the frailties of old age. Here one moment and into eternity with the Lord the next. What a blessing!

I can now pray with understanding and acceptance that simple phrase, *If I should die before I wake, I pray the Lord my soul to take.*

But without faith it is impossible to please him: for he that cometh to God must believe that he is, and that is a rewarder of them that diligently seek him. (Hebrews 11:6)

Taking In or Giving Out?

"It's not what you take in that makes the difference...it's what you give out," said P.K. Hallinan, a pastor and author of 70+ children's books. He was the featured speaker at an assembly honoring volunteer readers for the SMART (Start Making A Reader Today) program.

Hallinan went on to point out how important it is to give our time to help children learn to enjoy reading. He wanted to emphasize that we may not feel important, or even receive much credit or recognition. Nevertheless, we do make a difference. One story he told about a little girl named Annie revealed this to me more than any other. The next day I did some research on Anne's life.

Annie's story

Annie was born in April, 1866 near Springfield, Massachusetts into what we now call a dysfunctional family. Her parents were very poor Irish immigrants. Her father a drunk and her mother suffered from tuberculosis. When Annie was five years old, she contracted a disease of the eyes and because of the poor hygiene and not getting proper treatment, she gradually lost most of her vision.

She dreamed of happier days when she could escape her circumstances. After her mother died and her father unable to care for her and her brother, she lived with various relatives. Finally, she and her brother Jimmy were sent to the state charity "poorhouse" which meant she was now living with mentally ill people and prostitutes. Jimmy died there as a result of a congenital tubercular hip condition. All alone now, Annie continued to hold fast to her dream of one day going to school.

When an investigating committee visited the institution, Annie threw herself at their mercy, pleaded to be sent to a school for the blind. Since she could not read nor see clearly, she was somewhat handicapped when she arrived at Perkins Institute for the Blind in Boston. Although she was now 14 she had to start at the elementary level and her classmates often made fun of her. It was said she needed "taming" because of her lack of social skills and her rebellious attitude.

One teacher did see something worthwhile in Annie, however, and continued to show her love even when Annie was punished by being put in solitary confinement in the basement. Because of that teacher, Annie began to realize she could succeed in her desire to make something of herself. She graduated as valedictorian and the respect of her classmates at age 20. Annie chose to remain at the school to teach other children who were much like what she had once been.

Later, she was hired by a family with a little girl who was almost wild because of her frustration of not being able to see or hear. With patience and love, Annie was able to turn that child around to become the famous Helen Keller.

The application

The point of Hallinan's story was not how remarkable Annie turned out, nor Helen, but how we all recognize the names Anne Sullivan and Helen Keller but have never heard the name of the person who was responsible for saving Annie. He said, "That's how important each one is to every child to whom you read."

After hearing his talk, I've thought about what he said and how it relates to me. I thought about the writers' class I attend. Some members make the effort to write something to share and have critiqued by others, but many of us don't. We "take" but don't "give" of ourselves. Guilty feelings overwhelm me.

Another group I joined after retirement is a seniors' computer club. That's a different story because there I share what little I know to help those just learning computers. What a great feeling when someone remarks, "Thank you, I learned a lot today!"

As I continue to analyze how I spend my time, whether it's by "giving" or by "taking," I decided the Bible truth rang out loud and clear once again, **It's more blessed to give than to receive.** (Acts 20:35 KJV) Money isn't the only thing we have to give. Our time and talents are to be shared as well.

The Mystery of Courage

Many people call themselves Christians, but I am reminded of Christ's warning, *Not everyone that saith unto me, Lord, Lord, shall enter into the kingdom of heaven; but he that doeth the will of my Father which is in heaven.* (Matt 7:21) That not only would be a disappointment but a real tragedy!

A supposedly true story was told about an underground church in China (or perhaps Russia). As the members gathered for worship one morning, suddenly armed men broke in and shouted that they intended to kill anyone who professed to be a Christian. Those who did not wish to die and would refute his or her Christianity were allowed to leave. Most of the people present hurried out. Once they were gone, the 'killers' said, "Relax, everyone. The true believers are still here and now we can really worship!"

A scene such as that has, and continues to be, played out all around the world. How many of us who have never known such terror could be as courageous as those people? The question has been asked, "If you were arrested for being a Christian, would there be enough evidence to convict you?" In some countries today it takes courage to admit to being a Christian. Many of us heard the words of an American Iraqi woman who called a radio station during the war to say how glad she was that Iraq was finally going to be free. As a Christian, she had to flee her native country because she could not practice her faith.

The first American Christians who left everything behind to forge a new, free way of life here in America had courage to set sail on their unknown venture. Later on, it took courage for the pioneers to traverse the frontier, seeking more freedom.

A video about our Founding Fathers and how much emphasis they put on instilling Christian values into our laws *and* our schools is most interesting. Not only was our government established on the Judeo/Christian system, but all of the first elementary schools and nearly every college were started by and for Christians. The colleges required the enrollees to be believers in Christ, to read the scriptures daily and to have a prayer life. (Education and The Founding Fathers © 1991 by David Barton) Now, as I listen to the professors from Harvard, Yale and Princeton I wonder what the founders of those institutions would think if they could hear the garbage being spewed out today in those hallowed halls.

Some of the Founding Fathers were not always convinced the Christian way of life was the best, the only way. Noah Webster, the most famous of all lexicographers, was such a man. He was a brilliant lawyer who, in his later years, realized how wrong he had been by not leading and instilling Christian principles as the head of his family. All that had changed long before he died at age 85. When told he had little time left, it's said he quietly quoted, **I know Whom I have believed, and am persuaded that He is able to keep that which I have committed unto Him against that day,** (2 Timothy 1:12b) he peacefully closed his eyes and entered into eternity. (Education and The Founding Fathers © 1991 by David Barton)

While watching television during the Iraqi Freedom War, I was impressed by the courage our young men and women showed as they faced possible death. They believed in their cause and were willing to die for it. Likewise, those they fought against, especially the suicide bombers, believed in their purpose and willingly died. Over the centuries men have sincerely fought for their beliefs. Unfortunately, too many times they have been sincerely wrong and thus the suicide bombers died needlessly and entered into a Christless eternity. How sad for Jesus said, **I am the way, the truth, and the life: no man cometh unto the Father, but by me.** (John 14:6)

Missionaries, burdened by the fact that most of the world's population will meet with that same fate, oftentimes suffer insurmountable obstacles in order to bring the Saving Grace of Christ to the lost. Some have endured unbelievable hardships and others have died while serving.

People who suffer serious illnesses and maintain their faith and continue to hope for a better tomorrow are instilled with a different kind of courage. They refuse to give up. Medical science has been able to acquire new methods of treating some diseases because of these patients who keep on keeping on. They have been willing guinea pigs.

George Mueller was a man who started an orphanage when he could no longer stand to see the children going hungry. He didn't know where he would get the funds to feed and clothe them; he only knew he had to do something. The story is told about one morning when it was time to serve breakfast and there was nothing to eat. However, he told the children God would provide so they bowed in prayer. He no sooner finished his prayer and a knock came at the door. The food he had prayed for was there. He had faith, a lot of courage and the best part is, he acted on it!

Yes, courage is a mystery. Some have it; others don't. I thank God for those Christians who have it and prove it by their actions.

The Ultimate Sacrifice

Every adult has made some kind of a sacrifice at some point in life. Young newlyweds have been known to sacrifice by one of them putting education on hold while the other one obtains a desired degree. Sadly, some of those sacrifices end in divorce because the one who worked to pay expenses never "caught up" to the one who attained the educated status.

During the Great Depression, my father sacrificed by working on a farm away from the family so he could earn a pittance to send back to us. As circumstances improved and he returned home, every summer he spent hours putting in a large garden so our family would have enough food to keep from starving. He didn't have a motorized tractor to till his garden; rather, he developed a strong body with hard muscles by using a push plow. He wasn't the only one. That was the norm for that era. Mother and most other women canned to store up food for the winter. Sort of like the story of the ant in the Bible in Proverbs 6:6-8.

A great many parents make sacrifices to give their children advantages they themselves never had. Some are smart enough not to over give so their children can learn the meaning of hard work and rightly earn their own reward. Some parents, through good intentions, don't want their children to be deprived as they were and consequently, their offspring never learn a valuable lesson.

Our forefathers strove for freedom and all of the emblems of our history indicate that they looked to God Almighty for help. *Nowhere is this heritage seen more clearly than on the Liberty Bell. In 1751, the Pennsylvania Assembly called for the forging of a bell to commemorate William Penn's original charter of the state. They included instructions requiring that a Scripture verse be included on the bell. The verse is Leviticus 25:10, "Proclaim Liberty throughout all the land unto all the inhabitants thereof." Our Founding Fathers considered it important for all generations to know that God is the source of all our freedoms.*[1] The sacrifices they made are unnumbered, and too often these days unappreciated, so that we might continue to have freedom.

As one who dislikes, no hates, hot weather, I've been known to complain when the temperature gets over 90 degrees. Then I'm reminded of our troops who are willingly giving their utmost to keep us free. Many of them are serving in places where there are unbearable temperatures up to 140 degrees all the while burdened down with gear. Talk about sacrifice! The Bible tells us that **Greater love hath no man than this, that a man lay down his life for his friends**. (John 15:13) Our service people know this and continue to volunteer.

---

[1] Copied from Presidential Prayer Team Update for July 19, 2007

As noble as their actions are, no human being can die for another and thereby give them eternal life. But 2000+ years ago, one God/man did just that. He died that we might have eternal life. **For even the Son of man came not to be ministered unto, but to minister, and to give his life a ransom for many.** (Mark 10:45) That was Christ's sole purpose for leaving a glorious heaven and coming to earth as a human infant and later to be crucified.

No matter what sacrifices we make, none can ever compare to the ultimate sacrifice God made when he sent his Only Begotten Son to earth to be our Sacrificial Lamb.

Thy Kingdom Come

When Jesus taught his disciples to pray in Matthew 6:9-13, the phrase **Thy kingdom come. Thy will be done on earth, as it is in heaven** was included within the prayer. At the time the disciples thought Jesus came to establish a worldly kingdom. After all, they were oppressed by the Romans. They were looking for relief from the way they were being treated. What a disappointment it was when they later learned that Jesus would not release them from their woes. In fact, they learned that they would suffer even worse persecution.

The Internet is an interesting place to seek information but one must always remember that, just because it's there doesn't mean it's true. When searching for "kingdom" I discovered numerous sites that told about the "Kingdom of Heaven" and the "Kingdom of God." Since I'm not much of a movie-goer, I had not realized there have been books and movies on both subjects. There is also a website about a church which preaches about the "Kingdom."

In recent weeks we have witnessed and heard about one tragic shooting after another in crowded places, one even in a church. To think a church guard, who was armed, shot the shooter makes me wonder what this world is coming to when a church has a need for an armed guard.

An interesting email recently related how one

of the largest mega-churches in America has finished a study in which they discovered the important thing was to disciple...to teach and nurture...their people instead of striving for numbers. Well, DUH! Isn't that what Christ instructed in Matthew 28:19 & 20 just before he ascended into heaven? ***Go ye therefore and teach all nations, baptizing them in the name of the Father, and of the Son, and of the Holy Ghost: Teaching them to observe all things whatsoever I have commanded you: and, lo, I am with you always, even unto the end of the world. Amen.***

The leaders of the aforementioned mega-church cited Dr. Benjamin Spock who ruined a whole generation of children because parents followed his advice instead of the teachings of the Bible. They now believe they have not been true to the scriptures because they concentrated on gathering numbers instead of teaching the true gospel.

That brings me to the second part of the quotation from Christ's prayer: ***Thy will be done***. Isn't that where most of us have failed? We want "our" will, not Christ's. We simply are not willing to submit to His will.

To Chasten or Not

Well, here we are again...a New Year and time to make resolutions. I've made the same one for at least 50 years but because of a lack of discipline on my part it doesn't come to fruition. Discipline is extremely important to a Christian's life. We need to discipline ourselves about the way we take care of our bodies, how we support our church, how we treat others, and most of all, how obedient we are to God.

Our son was 21 years old when he told us, "I'm sure glad you guys were strict with me when I was growing up." I thanked him for realizing that and laughingly said, "Since we only had one child, we had to do it right the first time." It was true, both my husband and I were strict. In fact, my mother (who had been extremely strict when I was growing up) complained one day that, "I think you're too hard on Steve." That did make me laugh. We were fortunate in having a child who was basically good so needed little correction. I might add my own parents weren't that fortunate. I rebelled from the day I was born, I do believe.

Why did Steve tell us how grateful he was for his upbringing? Because he'd had one church friend who died of a drug overdose and another friend who intended becoming a missionary doctor but went "wild" once he got out on his own and away from legalistic parenting.

Throughout the Bible we read where God had to discipline the Israelites, or individuals, frequently. The psalmist tells us in Psalm 118:18 that **The Lord hath chastened me sore: but he hath not given me over unto death.** Many scriptures in Proverbs reveal how important discipline is. **Correction is grievous unto him that foresaketh the way: and he that hateth reproof shall die.** (Proverbs 15:10) **Chasten thy son while there is hope, and let not thy soul spare for his crying.** (Proverbs 19:18)

'Spare the rod and spoil the child' is a familiar saying. Does this mean a parent is to *beat* a child? By no means! Different personalities require different types of discipline. With some children the "look" is all it takes. My husband used to tell us that all his dad had to do when the four kids got a little too rambunctious in the house was lower his paper, peer over it and "look" at each child. They quickly calmed down. His dad never spanked them so there wasn't that fear. His father had trained them early on that some things were acceptable and others weren't.

Then, there is the child who refuses to mind no matter what. In my own way of thinking, such a child yearns to be noticed, to be loved. More often than not, that child is one who is hard to love because of his/her behavior. One of the new TV shows is called "Nanny 9-1-1". My granddaughter (who was about to become a mother for the first time) told me about it so I watched. It amazes me that grown adults have allowed their children to rule, and consequently, destroy a home's atmosphere.

In the episode I watched, two sets of parents had called "Nanny 9-1-1" for help because they had lost control of their children and everyone was suffering. It took the nannies one week to straighten out both homes. It all boiled down to the fact that there was no discipline!

The Apostle Paul wrote about orderliness in the church. **Let all things be done decently and in order.** (I Corinthians 14:40) In the book of Hebrews we read, **For whom the Lord loveth he chasteneth, and scourgeth every son whom he receiveth.** (Hebrews 12:6 KJV) In the Living Bible, the same verse reads, **For when he punishes you, it proves that he loves you. When he whips you it proves you are really his child.**

Yes, love...true Godly love...has to be the basis for discipline. A parent has to show the child there are guidelines to follow and when they aren't, there are consequences. Those of us who are no longer parenting still need to obey God's guidelines. For some of us, it may take our whole lifetime to accomplish this.

To Whom Honor Is Given

H**onor thy father and thy mother that thy days may be long** is the fifth commandment given by God to Moses. (Exodus 20:12) It is the first one with a promise and the first that deals with human behavior toward other humans. Yet, in today's world, it's easy to understand why some children don't honor their parents. Ever since drugs became a way of life, too many young parents have forfeited their responsibility. In some cases, grandparents have become the guardians of their grandchildren. Oftentimes, because of drugs, parents are downright cruel, physically and mentally, to their children. How can those children be expected to honor, much less love, a parent guilty of such treatment?

Not only are we to honor our parents but the Bible teaches us to **obey them that have the rule over you, and submit yourselves**. (Hebrews 13:17a) This is where I have a hard time because there are so many people in power who don't deserve any respect or honor.

A few years ago information came around about the lack of moral fiber among 535 individuals. They were guilty of behavior such as spousal abuse, fraud arrests, writing bad checks, bankrupting at least 2 businesses, doing time for assault, unable to obtain a credit card due to bad credit, drug-related charges, arrests for shoplifting, being defendants in lawsuits and arrests for drunk driving. The question was asked, "Were these athletes in the NFL or the AFL?" The correct answer was that they were the 535 men and women who composed the congress of the United States at that time.

While watching the hearings to confirm or reject a candidate for the Supreme Court, I had to ask myself how some of the senators could act so pious in light of their own actions. Is there no justice? The only way to show honor to such folk is to honor the position they hold and, *above all else, remember to pray for them.*

A Connecticut judge who gave a repeated rapist of a child a mere 60 days in jail does not deserve honor, in my humble opinion. Yet, he is a judge. God showed us how to deal with others when he told Moses, through his father-in-law, to set aside different numbers of groups and put people in place to rule over them, thus relieving Moses of the burden. (Exodus 18:13-27) The process isn't at fault. It's because of human frailty mistakes are made.

Whenever I see someone in uniform, I'm reminded of the oath he/she takes before joining any service. I am so thankful there are people who take their oath seriously and honorably live up to it! Where would America be if it weren't for them? That includes our police and fire personnel. They are needed and should be appreciated and honored.

Fortunately, there are people who are born to be gentle, good souls. They live their lives doing for others, thinking about what others may need, providing in any way they can to help someone else. That kind of person with innate goodness is too scarce.

Our local newspaper stirred up a hornet's nest when it ran a series of articles about beggars, especially "affluent beggars." It was the first I had heard the term "affluent beggar" although I worked in a welfare department for four years some fifty years ago. I know there are people who cheat to get something for nothing. That's sad because the Bible tells us we are to help those in need, those less fortunate than we. The Bible also tells us in , II Thessalonians 3:10 ***that if any would not work, neither should he eat***.

That's what bothers me about the beggars who like their lifestyle and don't want to work. Some people who could work simply find it easier to depend on others. I don't know anyone who isn't touched by someone truly in need and willing to help that person out of his dilemma. But, assisting someone who refuses to help him/herself is not scriptural.

So, back to the question, whom should we honor? Certainly, those who deserve it. But, who is it that deserves honor above everyone else? The first four commandments give us the answer... God. We are to have no other gods before Him; nor are we to make any graven idol to worship; nor take His Name in vain; and we are to remember the Sabbath day...to keep it holy. (Christians worship on Sunday.) In other words, we first and foremost must remember to honor God. We have seen what happens when we don't. Yet, we expect Him to remember us when we call out.

Victory Over Death

She was vibrant, loving life as a wife, mother and grandmother. On Friday she was joking with coworkers. By Sunday afternoon, she was gone from this life. Why, Lord? She had so much to live for. The shock of losing her is almost unbearable to those left behind. She wasn't sick, had no pain, no warning...until early Sunday morning. She wasn't feeling well and as she gradually got worse her husband decided she needed to see a doctor. He took her to the hospital and that's when they learned she was full of infection, evidently caused by a hole in her intestine.

We never know when our time on earth is up. Recently a friend, just one week short of her 104th year, passed away. She had been praying the Lord would take her for the past few years.

After watching loved ones die by inches because of a disease or live and not be cognizant of their surroundings and unable to participate as they once did, I've asked myself, is that better than having a loved one die suddenly? There is mourning and heartache in every instance. Just realizing you will never again see that person here on earth is a shock.

When an elderly person dies, we often think of it as a blessing, especially if there have been years of suffering. When a child or someone in the prime of life dies, there is excruciating heartache.

The Bible tells the story of Abraham, Lazarus and the rich man. While on earth, the rich man had much. Lazarus barely had crumbs. After death the rich man was experiencing torment and saw Lazarus on Abraham's bosom. He asked for mercy but was denied because he had passed all opportunities to repent while living. Then, the rich man asked if someone could go tell his brothers so they wouldn't make the same mistake. He was told, **If they do not listen to Moses and the Prophets neither will they be persuaded if someone rises from the dead.** (Luke 16:19-31)

In recent years we have heard stories about people who have "died" and returned to tell of their experience either in heaven or hell. Their new life is better than it ever was before because of the peace and assurance they gained. They also have an urgency to reach others for Christ...to convince them there is life after death. Perhaps this is God's way in trying to reach the lost because time is growing short.

Anyone's death is sad if he/she has refused to accept Christ's gift of eternal life. For the Christian, we find peace and comfort in knowing that there will come a time when we will be reunited with our loved ones *if* they also knew Christ and accepted his gift while in this world. There is victory through Jesus because of his sacrifice. He came as a babe to share in our humanity. He died for our sins and rose to new life, conquering death.

The Lord gives and the Lord takes...but in His time. Our job is to be ready whenever our time on earth is up. ***Now is the day of salvation.*** (2 Corinthians 6:2)

What Is Truth?

Is truth what you believe or what I believe, based on our knowledge from life's experiences? I don't think so. There is a radio talk show host who begins his program with, "You shall know the truth and the truth shall make you mad!" Those of us who remember a similar verse from the Bible know another ending that states, **You shall know the truth and the truth shall make you free.** (John 8:32) In each case, I believe the word 'truth' is referring to two different entities.

The radio host refers to all the "stuff" going on in our world today, political and social inequities that he does not hesitate to mention day in and day out.

In John 8:32 Jesus is talking about being free from sin. He makes that clear as he explains to his disciples in verse 36. **If the Son therefore shall make you free, ye shall be free indeed!"**

It used to be before a witness was sworn in to testify, he put his left hand on the Bible and raised his right hand affirming to, "Tell the truth, the whole truth, and nothing but the truth, *so help me God."* Those last four words have been dropped in recent years in many courts.

Because our schools have been lax in teaching how our country was established, few people know the truth about how important religion was to our Founding Fathers in establishing our laws and system of government. That may be the reason we are losing the moral foundation on which this nation was built.

Back in Old Testament times, Moses told the parents that he was giving them the commandments to put upon their hearts. Furthermore, he told them, ***Impress them on your children. Talk about them when you sit at home and when you walk along the road, when you lie down and when you get up. Tie them as symbols on your hands and bind them on your foreheads. Write them on the doorframes of your houses and on your gates.*** (Deuteronomy 6:7-9) In other words, make them a part of your every being and your children's. More often than not today we leave it up to Sunday school teachers and ministers to tell our children and us right from wrong.

In The Daily Walk devotional book for February 22, 2006, it discussed Moses and how he was instructing parents to teach their children. They printed an ad that read: "WANTED – Energetic, young couple for demanding assignment. Must have boundless reserves of patience, stamina, and optimism. Must be able to function reasonably well on three hours of sleep, diagnose childhood ailments, and read the same book twenty-seven times without appearing bored. Must together be skilled as a nurse, counselor, teacher, and taxi cab driver. Full-time position. No paid vacations.

Salary not commensurate with experience. Those applying will be screened to determine their sanity!"

Who would ever want such a job because it sure isn't easy? Fortunately, a lot of people do as the rewards outnumber the inconveniences many times over. There is nothing that takes the place of the bond of love we humans have for one another except the love of God for us.

So, what is truth? Well, according to humans, it can be integrity, honesty, sincerity, candor, frankness, uprightness, virtue, fidelity, openness, genuineness, accuracy, exactness, precision, reality and verity, all to some degree. But, none of them compare with the **truth that makes us free** once we turn our lives over to Christ.

What Purpose?

Ever since Rick Warren wrote his book, *The Purpose Driven Church*, Christians have been discussing their purpose. But, that is not a new concept. From the beginning of mankind we know that man was created for one purpose and that is to love and honor God, our Creator. The preacher of Ecclesiastes, after writing about the vanity of man, ends his dialogue with these words: **Let us hear the conclusion of the whole matter: Fear God, and keep his commandments; for this is the whole duty of man.** (Ecclesiastes 12:13) Yet, how often do we hear someone who is dwelling and sinking in self-pity utter, "Why am I here? What good am I to anyone?"

Getting discouraged from time to time is a normal process for someone who is going full speed ahead and then hitting ruts in the road. This happens to parents often when their last child leaves the nest. Years ago when mothers stayed home it was more of a problem because their whole purpose in life was taking care of their children's needs. Once that need was gone, they didn't know what to do with all the extra time. How well I remember going through a depression time when all who needed my help and care were gone. It was easy to think, *What now, Lord?*

Today with women working outside the home,

it's almost a relief when they have less responsibility. But, therein lies one of the problems we have. Children have been raised without proper supervision and thus allowed too much freedom.

So, what's the solution for finding a new purpose? Once our family responsibility is gone, is it now our turn to have fun? It could be. I smile whenever I see the sign on the back of an RV that says, *We're spending our kids' inheritance* or something similar. There's a lot of this world to see once we leave our own little corner.

Believing there are three dimensions for the human...mind, body and soul...it is important to take care of all. Traveling is one way to expand our mind. We learn about other people and that's good. Furthering one's education is another way to develop our mind.

One can't turn on the TV or open a magazine or newspaper without being bombarded by diet and exercise commercials. We spend fortunes on our bodies. Some are successful in keeping in shape well into their elder years. Some are not, even in their early years.

That leaves the soul which seems to be the least cared for of the three dimensions. It's been said an older person reads his Bible more frequently because he's cramming for his finals. What a tragedy because that's exactly where we find the answers to life's dilemmas. The Bible tells us many times that, if we turn to God, he will direct our path. Matthew wrote, **Seek ye first the kingdom of God and his righteousness; and all these things will be added unto you.** (Matthew 6:33)

Recently I learned another meaning for the word "purpose" when I put my home up for sale. When I asked what I should do to make it more presentable, the realtor said, "Get rid of any clutter." Now, I don't like clutter so I was surprised she mentioned it. She pointed to my kitchen counter where I had a habit of stacking my "hands on" stuff. That afternoon I got busy and cleared it away as well as removing all the 'stickums' on the refrigerator. I was amazed that evening when I glanced out to see what looked like a bare kitchen.

Believe me, when you put your house on the market, it gives you a purpose to do some thorough cleaning out. Although I'm not a diehard packrat, I fall somewhere in between that and the person who manages to live with few mementos. I'm one who believes you never need something until you give or throw it away.

So, back to the question of *What Purpose?* because everyone needs a purpose, a goal. For the Christians that purpose should be to live our lives so that others will want the joy and peace we have in Christ.

Worship the King

"O Worship the King" is the first hymn in one of my songbooks. A good way to start a worship hymnal. On the back page are the "Doxology" and "Gloria Patri". All three hymns were sung often when I was growing up. The last two were sung every Sunday; the first after the offering was taken and the latter at the beginning of the service. We stood as if we were soldiers at attention.

Sir Robert H. Grant, who lived from 1779-1838, penned the words to "O, Worship the King". Johann Haydn arranged the tune, LYONS, to the song we still sing today but not often. For some of us old-timers, it's been difficult to accept the more leisurely method of worshiping. Too informal. But, we are trying and even getting into the swing of it...to a degree. When I watch videos of Africans singing praises their whole body moves and their arms are held high, praising the Lord. The Bible tells how the Israelites raised their hands as they worshiped God so that type of worship has been around a lot longer than I but old habits are hard to break.

Many of us seniors have been criticized because we seemingly remain stiff and aloof to the modern ways of worship. Those who criticize do have a point. Some seniors can attend a sports game and go crazy with excitement. Why can't we be as enthusiastic for the Lord?

Well, give us time. We are gradually coming around to realizing that "*Happiness is the Lord*" and we're learning to show it.

Too many churches have been hurt, even split, over methods of worshiping, especially when it comes to the song service. A little bending on each side would help. None of the "My way or the highway" thinking, however, as it accomplishes nothing but more dissent. The Bible teaches us to do **all things in moderation**. (Philippians 4:5) Those of us who were raised in the more sedate type of worshiping must be willing to accept the modern, less formal type. Likewise, the younger folk need to be willing to accept some of our old favorites. To me, an excellent worship service consists of both types of songs.

One thing older people may not take into account is that many of the praise songs today are words directly from scripture. We need to remember that the longest book in the Bible is Psalms...all praises to God.

Singing is only one part of worship. I believe prayer is an essential aspect of any worship service. I attended a funeral service for a neighbor years ago at a cult-type of church. Not one prayer was uttered. What a tragedy, I thought.

The Bible tells us to fellowship with one another. Where better to do that than at church? A favorite Bible verse is Psalm 46:10 which states, **Be still and know that I am God**.

Oftentimes I've heard the question asked, "Why was I born?" The answer is found at the end of Ecclesiastes 12:13. **Let us hear the conclusion of the whole matter: Fear God, and keep his commandments: for this is the whole duty of man.**

If that's true, and I believe it is, we humans have gone astray with our worshiping things and other people. I cannot fathom the idol worship of another human being. Yet, sports figures and entertainers are adored beyond measure. People, including Christians, pay hard-earned money just to see them. What a shame! If some of those people were asked to tithe to their church, I wonder if they would consider that a privilege or be willing to make a sacrifice.

There are those who put their possessions ahead of everything else. Too people treasure their belongings even over family. It's quite true that **where your treasure is, there will your heart be also**. (Matthew 6:21) Something has happened to our priorities.

One verse of "O, Worship the King" sums up our station in life and our relationship to God very well.

Frail children of dust, and feeble as frail,
In Thee do we trust, nor find Thee to fail;
Thy mercies how tender! How firm to the end!
Our Maker, Defender, Redeemer and Friend.

www.ingramcontent.com/pod-product-compliance
Lightning Source LLC
Chambersburg PA
CBHW032251150426
43195CB00008BA/404